THE EVERYTHING®

Weddings on a Budget Book, 2nd Edition

Dear Reader,

I'm so glad that you've chosen this book to help you plan your wedding! Whether your budget is modest or large, you've chosen this book to help you plan your wedding because you want to spend wisely. Working with a wedding budget may be the first time the two of you will be discussing and handling finances together. It can be a terrific learning experience, one that will pave the way for a great future together.

It might be hard to believe you can avoid overextending yourself when you plan something as important as a wedding, but helping you stay within your budget is what this book is all about. You will discover that it's possible to have a lovely wedding on far less money than you think—without compromising what's important to you.

Perhaps you want to spend more on some aspect of your wedding than the "experts" say you should. This book will show you how to do it without harming your overall budget. It also has advice for saving as much as possible on your overall wedding expenses to allow for a nicer honeymoon or for making a down payment for your first house. Do what makes you happy, and don't go by anyone else's rules. It's your wedding and your life.

Barbara

The EVERYTHING® Series

These handy, accessible books give you all you need to tackle a difficult project, gain a new hobby, or even brush up on something you learned back in school but have since forgotten. You can read cover to cover or just pick out information from the four useful boxes.

 Alerts: Urgent warnings

 Essentials: Quick and handy tips

 Facts: Important sound bytes of information

 Questions: Solutions to common problems

Now you can finally say you know *Everything*®!

EDITORIAL

Director of Innovation: Paula Munier
Editorial Director: Laura M. Daly
Executive Editor, Series Books: Brielle K. Matson
Associate Copy Chief: Sheila Zwiebel
Acquisitions Editor: Kerry Smith
Associate Development Editor: Elizabeth Kassab
Production Editor: Casey Ebert

PRODUCTION

Director of Manufacturing: Susan Beale
Production Project Manager: Michelle Roy Kelly
Prepress: Erick DaCosta, Matt LeBlanc
Managing Designer: Heather Blank
Interior Layout: Heather Barrett,
Brewster Brownville, Colleen Cunningham

Visit the entire Everything® series at www.everything.com

THE
EVERYTHING
WEDDINGS®
ON A BUDGET
BOOK

2nd Edition

Plan the wedding of your dreams—
without going bankrupt!

Barbara Cameron

▲adams media
Avon, Massachusetts

To Sarah

An Everything® Series Book.
Everything® and everything.com® are registered
trademarks of F+W Publications, Inc.

Published by Adams Media, an F+W Publications Company
57 Littlefield Street, Avon, MA 02322 U.S.A.
www.adamsmedia.com

ISBN-10: 1-59869-418-9
ISBN-13: 978-1-59869-418-5

Printed in Canada.

J I H G F E D C B A

Library of Congress Cataloging-in-Publication Data
Cameron, Barbara
The everything weddings on a budget book
/ Barbara Cameron. – 2nd ed.
p. cm. – (An everything series book)
Includes index.
ISBN-13: 978-1-59869-418-5 (pbk.)
ISBN-10: 1-59869-418-9 (pbk.)
1. Weddings–Planning. 2. Wedding etiquette.
3. Budgets, Personal. I. Title.

HQ745.C35 2007
395.2'2–dc22
2007030944

This publication is designed to provide accurate and authoritative information with regard to the subject matter covered. It is sold with the understanding that the publisher is not engaged in rendering legal, accounting, or other
professional advice. If legal advice or other expert assistance is required, the
services of a competent professional person should be sought.

—From a *Declaration of Principles* jointly adopted by a Committee of the
American Bar Association and a Committee of Publishers and Associations

Many of the designations used by manufacturers and sellers to distinguish
their products are claimed as trademarks. Where those designations appear
in this book and Adams Media was aware of a trademark claim, the designations have been printed with initial capital letters.

This book is available at quantity discounts for bulk purchases.
For information, please call 1-800-289-0963.

Contents

Acknowledgments

Thanks to my editor, Kerry Smith, for asking me to update this book and for offering great suggestions and direction. Thanks, too, to the many brides, grooms, and others who shared their stories with me.

The Top Ten Ways to Plan a Luxurious and Affordable Wedding

1. Talk—often! The more you and your fiancé talk and come to an agreement about money matters, the better.

2. Don't think of your budget as a constraint. Think of it as an opportunity and a challenge.

3. Reward yourself for coming in under budget with small, affordable luxuries.

4. Avoid impulse purchases.

5. Put the money for wedding expenses in its own account.

6. Request overdraft protection on the wedding account.

7. Use a low-interest credit card that offers frequent-flyer miles for each wedding purchase made.

8. Look for ways to save by doing certain jobs yourself instead of assigning others.

9. Comparison shop.

10. Consider free credit-counseling services if necessary.

Introduction

You're engaged and planning your wedding—what a wonderful time in your life! It's exciting to plan a day you may have been looking forward to for a long time. There are so many plans buzzing in your head, so many things to do and buy and arrange, and you feel like spending whatever it takes to have what you want.

That's exactly how the people in the wedding business hope you're feeling. There are hundreds of businesses, books, magazines, and Web sites out there just waiting to tell you all the things you need and how much you'll have to spend to get them. While it's tempting to blithely and blindly spend your way to the altar, you need to think carefully about the future to avoid starting your married life with financial problems.

You might feel that budgeting your wedding takes the fun, romance, and excitement out of planning the most important day of your life. Not true! But feeling taken advantage of and going broke truly will take the romance out of your big day.

That's why *The Everything® Weddings on a Budget Book, 2nd Edition* is exactly what you need. It will guide you to the particular budget that will work for you and help you spend wisely to have the wedding and honeymoon of your dreams. Being on a budget does not mean you're skimping or settling for second best. A budget is simply a thought-out plan for spending wisely, no matter how much or how little money is involved. Even celebrity couples planning their weddings in Italian castles establish a budget.

Today, most couples and their families and friends have busy, busy lives. They don't have time to run around and investigate a dozen venues and stores to save money. That's why *The Everything® Weddings on a Budget Book, 2nd Edition* includes ways to save time as well as money. After all, you want to be able to live your life while you're planning the next step in it. Wedding and honeymoon planning can't be all you do and think about for months on end!

This updated second edition is filled with new practical advice as well as more budgeting and time worksheets. It includes suggestions from many brides, their friends, relatives, parents, and wedding professionals. With their help you, too, can make your wedding and honeymoon dreams come true.

Chapter 1
Making a Budget

You've seen those articles in magazines and newspapers reporting that the "average" wedding costs nearly $30,000 these days. Oh, really? Maybe when you average in the outrageous amounts spent by celebrities. In any case, the statistics don't matter. You choose the amount that is appropriate for your budget and then find ways to make your special day priceless.

Budget Is a Good Word—Really!

What's a budget, you ask? If you've never put together a budget plan, let alone stuck to one, this chapter is crucial to your financial health, both in preparation for your wedding and for years to come.

A Budget: Defined

budg•et (bŭj´ĭt) *n* The total sum of money allocated for a particular purpose or period of time.

Notice that the fine folks at the *American Heritage Dictionary* don't equate budgeting with deprivation.

 Essential

> Think about the sense of satisfaction and accomplishment you'll feel if you set a budget and bring in the wedding expenses within that budget. Daily living within your paycheck is a good skill to learn for making big purchases like a future home or new car.

Perhaps you already keep a monthly budget, planning for living expenses and budgeting for the unexpected. A wedding budget is very similar—a plan for expected and unexpected expenditures. If you're already a budgeter, you'll feel at home with the process, and if you're a first-timer, this may be the start of a new way of looking at how you spend.

It's Not (Just) About the Money

Money is a topic fraught with potential emotional issues and stress. How you and your fiancé plan for the first expenses of your life together will set the stage for harmony in your relationship. There will never be a time when it is more important to make a realistic budget without emptying the checking account, maxing out your credit cards, or, if they're paying, upsetting either set of parents over out-of-control spending.

The First Step

Knowing what each of you wants is the first step in planning your wedding. Grab your fiancé, find a comfortable seat, and take this easy quiz together. It will help the two of you determine your budget and better plan for this special day.

Plan Your Wedding: A Quiz

1. Where do you want to hold the wedding ceremony?
   a. church
   b. outdoor location (such as a park)
   c. home
   d. destination wedding
   e. mansion or a historical site
   f. other _____

2. Where do you want to hold the reception?
   a. church hall
   b. hotel
   c. country club
   d. resort
   e. fellowship hall or community center
   f. other _____

3. How many people will you invite?
   a. 5–25
   b. 25–50
   c. 50–100
   d. 100+

4. How much can you spend on the wedding and reception?
   a. up to $2,000
   b. $2,001–$10,000
   c. $10,001–$20,000
   d. $20,000+

5. Who will pay for the wedding and reception?
   a. bride's parents
   b. groom's parents
   c. bride and groom's parents
   d. bride and groom

6. If you are paying for all or part of the wedding, how will you pay for it?
   a. savings
   b. loan

    c. credit cards

    d. a combination of the above

7. What tasks will you undertake for the wedding?
    a. ceremony planning
    b. reception planning
    c. invitations
    d. decorations, favors, gifts
    e. music
    f. transportation
    g. food, cake, beverages
    h. flowers
    i. photography
    j. wedding Web site
    k. honeymoon planning
    l. other _____

8. How much will you spend on a honeymoon?
    a. up to $1,000
    b. $1,001–$3,000
    c. $3,000+

9. Where will you go for a honeymoon?
    a. bed-and-breakfast in the United States
    b. all-inclusive resort in the Caribbean
    c. luxurious hotel overseas
    d. camping at a nature destination
    e. other _____

10. For which types of things will you register to set up your new home?
    a. household items
    b. bed and bath items
    c. electronic gifts (television, microwave, stereo, camera, etc.)
    d. honeymoon registry
    e. other _____

Once the two of you figure out what you want and how you envision your wedding, you can begin to plan all the details—including, of course, the budget.

Your Preliminary Overall Financial Budget

You know you're perfect for each other over the long haul, but what did you discover after taking the wedding-planning quiz? Were your ideas and dreams for the wedding alike or did they seem miles apart? Certainly even the most compatible couple can have wildly different visions of their wedding day and its price tag. Whether you have different expectations based on the wedding you've always imagined or different priorities in your plans for the future, be prepared for wedding planning to require communication and compromise. It's a genuine team effort.

What Did the Quiz Reveal?

Did you discover major differences between the total amounts you each want to spend or in the way you want to pay for your wedding day? Perhaps one of you wants to finance a big fancy wedding with a credit card, an idea that makes the other person ready to faint.

Such differences in opinion are easier to overcome than you might think. By making a budget, you can decide on your priorities and spend money on them instead of letting money dribble out for items that aren't as important. When you know you have less to spend on other things, you can find ways to save instead of automatically increasing your spending.

Decide Now What's Most Important

Ask yourselves which features of the wedding are important to you. Each of you should make a list and star the two or three items that are the most important. Is it the ceremony itself? The reception? The wedding dress? Flowers? Think about it.

Compare your two lists. How closely do you and your fiancé agree on the big expenditures?

 Fact

In wedding budgets, there is the reception, and then there is everything else. The reception can cost up to 50 percent of the total budget. This includes the price of renting the reception hall or space itself as well as providing food and beverages for your guests.

Which two or three features matter most to you? Let's say you've picked the dress, the flowers, and the reception.

Your fiancé is most concerned about the reception and the music. Now you know you'll need to figure out some compromises and decide where to focus money and time within your budget.

Check your lists to see whether you left off any potential wedding expenses. Omissions may point to areas that neither of you rate as a priority, and you can start your savings there. For instance, if neither of you mentioned the honeymoon, you may be able to save money by opting for a less expensive locale.

Putting Your Heads Together

Now it's time to get together with those involved in footing the bill for the wedding and reception. Is the bride's family paying or is the groom's? Are you, as a couple, paying for it yourselves? Many couples are getting married later these days and they are financially secure enough to pay for their own wedding. They want to make decisions themselves without input or interference from parents. Today there are no rules for who pays.

 Alert

Make sure each financially involved party gives you a firm dollar amount. Hashing out details now might be uncomfortable, but it will save you from the anguish of a potentially disastrous misunderstanding later.

Are There Strings Attached to the Money?

If your family is paying, ask how much they are willing to spend. How flexible is their offer? Can they adjust the amount for unforeseen expenses? Work out how your family will transfer the money to you and when it will be available.

 Essential

More and more couples are paying for their own weddings. The latest studies show that 32 percent of couples now pay for their own nuptials. An estimated 30 percent of brides' parents pay for the wedding, according to Condé Nast Bridal Group.

Remember that when others are helping to foot the bill, they usually feel they have something to say about how the money is spent. You and your fiancé have to carefully consider the hidden costs of accepting money if you feel there may be problems. Your wedding—and the planning that goes into it—is supposed to be a joyous occasion, not one fraught with controversy and conflict. You may have to choose your battles. If there are ongoing disagreements, decide what you absolutely must have and weigh it against your family's financial help. You may find that some things aren't as important as you thought.

If you and your fiancé are paying for your own wedding, how will you make it work? First, set up a joint account just for the wedding. Having a wedding-specific account will help you keep track of how much you have spent and how much you have left.

Three Budget Categories

All couples have varying financial resources and differing expectations for their wedding. That said, it's still important for you to get a feel for some general guidelines. Follow three couples as they plan their budgets.

 Fact

Wedding expenses are on the rise. Nearly every aspect of the wedding has increased more than 20 percent since 2002, according to CNNMoney.com. The site reports that the average amount spent on a wedding is now at $27,852, up 100 percent since 1990.

A Modest Budget

Susan and her fiancé Nick are planning a modest wedding with about two dozen friends and family members. They're college sweethearts who are about to graduate. Because their parents helped a lot with college, Susan and Nick don't want to ask them to pay for the wedding. They are both starting new jobs, so they don't have much money or time. Together they have established an objective of saving on wedding expenses so they can put a down payment on a house in the near future and begin paying off some student loans.

In spite of their long-term financial goals, there's no need for Susan and Nick to feel they are compromising on the quality of their wedding. According to Susan, "When it really comes down to it, Nick and I don't want a lavish wedding. We'll just have those people who are really special with us on our wedding day." They'd like to hold their expenses under $5,000. Theirs is a modest budget.

A Moderate Budget

Kylie's parents are paying for her wedding. They're working with a budget of approximately $20,000. Her fiancé's parents may pick up a few traditional expenses as well. Nevertheless, Kylie and Sean are staying conscious of expenses; they don't want their parents to feel strained. Let's call their budget moderate.

A Luxurious Wedding

Lynn and her fiancé, John, have been living together and sharing expenses for the past two years, and they command high salaries for their careers as real-estate consultants. Together, Lynn and John have set up a checking account with $50,000 designated for wedding expenses.

"We want to celebrate our wedding day with a big party and invite all our friends and some business associates," Lynn explained. "Our jobs are dynamic and our days are long, so I'm hiring a wedding consultant to help me plan the wedding. We're pulling out all the stops to have a lavish, elegant day." Lynn and John's budget can be called luxurious.

What's Your Budget?

First, sit down and decide how much you can spend. That's your bottom figure. Then decide how much you could stretch that if you had to. Your budget must include a substantial cushion to cover any miscellaneous or unexpected expenses. Even if you are a strict budgeter, plan for a certain amount—what you feel you can afford—for unexpected expenditures.

Given your own sense of how much money is "a lot" as well as what you've read in magazines or heard from friends, determine which category your budget falls into: modest, moderate, or luxurious.

Of course, what these categories really mean will be different depending on which part of the country you're in and the locale of your wedding. For example, a budget some would consider moderate in Crossett, Arkansas, could be termed modest in Atlanta, Georgia. However, large cities may give you more options for a less expensive wedding. Small towns may have only one vendor for a wedding gown and one photographer. Be aware that you may incur additional expenses for travel time—either because you have to drive to a bigger city to find what you want or because you choose more distant vendors to come to you.

The Latest Tips for Budget Success

Perhaps you've heard the statistic that 50 percent of all marriages in the United States end in divorce. Experts debate that statistic, saying it's misleading to compare the new marriages in a given year with the total number of divorces filed. However, the fact is that most divorced couples report money problems as a large factor in the failure of their relationship.

Plan for the Future

Think of your wedding budget as one of the first times you and your fiancé will discuss your attitudes about money, plan expenditures, and work together to execute your plan. It's the perfect place to lay a strong foundation for a successful financial union. Even if one of you is doing most of the planning and spending, it's important that you both agree on how this will be done. That spirit of budgetary responsibility will reflect itself in marital harmony.

 Fact

Always ask if you qualify for a discount. There are discounts for students, senior citizens, AAA members, and repeat customers. Some vendors also give you a discount if you work in a certain business or profession.

Making your financial decisions—for the wedding and for life—through discussion, compromise, and sound budget principles will set you up for success. Apply these principles to your wedding expenses, and you will know what to expect for your financial future together.

What Is Your Money Personality?

People deal with money in vastly different ways. It helps to figure out how you and your fiancé each handle money and how your strategies differ. From there you can work together to find a way to handle your finances in a way that suits both of you. Most people are a combination of the following personality types:

- **Impulsive Spender:** A stressful day at the office drives you to frivolous spending at the mall or an expensive dinner at a restaurant on the way home. You feel you work hard and deserve to have what you want. After all, you only live once.
- **Frugal (Non-)Spender:** Save, save, save! You adhere to the philosophy that you never know when you might need some extra cash. You find it hard to spend money, and you give every potential purchase so much thought that others squirm when they're out shopping with you.
- **Bingeing Consumer:** You save money for a long time, then go on a spending spree.
- **Ostrich:** You avoid thinking about money. You spend it, of course, but you don't keep a balanced checkbook, and you have made a few financial missteps that have cost you in late fees or other penalties.
- **Worrier:** You stress over your finances constantly. You are meticulous about organizing financial records, paying your bills on time, and keeping your checkbook balanced.

It's hardest—but not impossible—for two extremes to work together. For example, impulsive spenders and frugal spenders who marry face challenges simply because their attitudes toward money vary so drastically. In any case, be sensitive to your fiancé's money personality as the two of you plan your wedding together.

Personal Stories

"My parents are divorced," recounts Susan, "and I can remember hearing a lot of arguments about money. I don't want that with Nick, so we've done a lot of talking about how we'll deal with money issues when we're married. We're not going to get into a lot of debt to get married—partly because we want a house within the next year or two, and partly because we feel like we've already gotten into a lot of debt getting our college degrees. We hope we'll have good jobs very soon, but we do want to be careful."

Kylie's parents have a long-lasting marriage and are co-owners of a business. They make money decisions in both their marriage and their business with ease. Sean's parents often disagree about how to spend money; however, they find ways to compromise. Both Kylie and Sean feel their parents have been good role models for how couples should handle money.

Question?

How can I prevent impulsive purchases or financial commitments?
Before making a purchase for your wedding, ask yourself if you really need the item, or if you just want it. Make it a rule to think about it overnight and see how you feel the next day.

Lynn reports that she often heads to the mall or tunes in to the TV shopping channels when she's had an unusually tiring and stressful day. She has had to consciously work on not making impulsive purchases.

"John tends to make impulsive purchases, too, but it happens more because he sees a good deal, not because he's stressed," Lynn says. "I don't think either of us makes decisions about money based on how our parents handled money issues. I think it's more that we have to have a faster-paced way of making money decisions given our careers and the work that we do."

Lynn also knows that despite having money set aside for a lavish wedding, expenses can spiral out of control if she falls into her habitual pattern of spending impulsively when she's tired and stressed.

Susan and Nick, Kylie and Sean, and Lynn and John all understand how their attitudes toward money will affect their wedding planning and their lives together. Lynn recognizes her spending personality and knows how it can affect the wedding budget. The other couples realize that communication is the key to making their budgets work.

Wedding Budget Worksheet

Use this worksheet to document expenses for your wedding. Keeping track of everything you spend ensures that you stay within your budget. Make a copy of the worksheet and tuck it into your purse or daily calendar so you remember to record entries as soon as you make purchases. You might need to customize this worksheet a bit, depending on your particular wedding plans.

Wedding consultant:	$_____
Ceremony site fee:	$_____
Reception site food and beverages:	$_____

Bridal attire

Dress:	$_____
Headpiece:	$_____
Shoes:	$_____
Undergarments and pantyhose:	$_____
Hairdresser and makeup:	$_____
Miscellaneous:	$_____

Groom's attire

Tuxedo rental or purchase:	$_____
Shoes:	$_____
Underwear and socks:	$_____
Miscellaneous:	$_____

Stationery and postage

Save-the-date cards: $_____

Invitations: $_____

Thank-you cards: $_____

Programs: $_____

Postage: $_____

Miscellaneous: $_____

Flowers

Bridal bouquet: $_____

Attendants' bouquets: $_____

Corsages and
boutonnieres: $_____

Ceremony site flowers
and decorations: $_____

Reception site flowers
and decorations: $_____

Miscellaneous flowers
and decorations: $_____

Music

Ceremony site music: $_____

Reception site music: $_____

Other:

Wedding cake: $_____

Transportation: $_____

Photography: $_____

Videography: $_____

Wedding favors and frills: $_____

Wedding party gifts:	$_____
Tips:	$_____
Miscellaneous:	$_____

Fees

Officiant:	$_____
Marriage license:	$_____
Blood tests:	$_____

Miscellaneous

Wedding insurance:	$_____
Wedding party expenses (hotel, airfare, etc.):	$_____
Wedding Web site:	$_____
Entertainment expenses for out-of-town guests:	$_____
Engagement dinner:	$_____
Rehearsal dinner:	$_____
Utensils (cake knife, toasting flutes, etc.):	$_____

Honeymoon

Airfare:	$_____
Car rental:	$_____
Accommodations:	$_____
Food:	$_____
Entertainment:	$_____
Travel insurance:	$_____
Miscellaneous:	$_____

Total: **$_____**

Chapter 2
Carrying Out
Your Plans

Now that you know what you want and what you can afford, it's time to create a plan to convert your wishes to reality. You may have to get creative to reach all of your goals, and the least-expensive route is not always obvious. This chapter gets you started; subsequent chapters help you deal with particular issues in greater detail.

Getting Started

There's so much to remember as you plan your wedding. Feeling overwhelmed? Relax! This list of what you need can help you feel more in control.

 Essential

The groom's family traditionally pays for certain expenses, such as the marriage license, wedding officiant's fee, the bride's bouquet and going-away corsage, the rehearsal dinner, the honeymoon, and some lodging expenses.

Regardless of whether you are planning a modest, moderate, or luxurious wedding, you need to account for the basics. Typical planned expenditures include the following:

- Invitations, stationery, and programs
- Bride's wedding gown, alterations, and accessories
- Groom's attire
- Flowers
- Ceremony location
- Reception location
- Catering
- Ceremony music
- Reception music
- Photography
- Videography
- Transportation
- Wedding rings

- Marriage license
- Blood tests
- Officiant's fee
- Attendants' gifts
- Rehearsal dinner
- Honeymoon

You may not require all of these for your own wedding, so keep that in mind as you prioritize what you need and want. You can use the worksheets in this book to help you manage your wedding budget or easily use a spreadsheet to keep a master ledger of transactions. Create your own or use a budget calculator at *www.theknot.com* or *www.weddingchannel.com*.

The Big Two

Typically, the two most important factors in determining the cost of a wedding are the size of the guest list and the location. Begin the planning process by answering the following two questions:

- How many guests will you invite? Since the reception often costs up to half of the final cost of the wedding, knowing the number of guests to plan for is crucial right from the beginning.
- Where will the wedding and reception take place? Wedding and reception venues vary widely in price, so narrowing (or nailing down)

your choices as soon as possible is essential for budgeting and planning.

Alert

The size of the party and location of the wedding require the biggest part of your wedding budget and make a difference in how much money you have left over for other expenses, like your wedding gown or the photographer.

During the months of planning, it's important to stick to a set number of guests and not let the guest list mushroom, because that will make your total expenses rise.

Preliminary Time Budget Planning

An important part of laying out a plan for yourself is in budgeting your time. The adage that time is money is especially true these days. Sure, you could save money by doing most things for your wedding yourself. But do you really want to be up late the night before your ceremony affixing flowers to a wedding canopy, writing out a seating chart, and folding napkins into swans? Not only will you look stressed and haggard the next day, you will feel it, and you'll miss out on enjoying the perfect experience you've both worked so hard to create.

With everything you have to do, it may be worth the financial investment to have as many arrangements and details as possible taken care of by others. The basic strategy is one of delegation.

Then, too, the better you organize your time, the more you will have to spend looking for bargains and arranging realistic delivery dates. You don't want to hear that charges are doubled because last-minute orders require surcharges for express delivery or extra manpower. Making a time budget—and keeping it in a prominent place—saves time and money.

Hiring a Wedding Consultant

Another big time saver—and, in some cases, a money saver—is to hire a wedding consultant. Some consultants charge a flat fee; others charge a percentage of the wedding budget (typically 10 to 15 percent). Be sure to clarify fees before you make a final decision about the person you hire, but don't base your decision on the fee alone. Consider how much you plan on having the consultant do for you. Keep in mind that good consultants usually have working relationships with excellent vendors and venues that can translate into opportunities for savings.

 Fact

Wedding consultants don't just save you time and money—they can save you wear and tear on the nerves. Your consultant has firsthand experience with the trials and tribulations of working with wedding families as well as with vendors.

What Can You Do for Me?

Time is probably the most important factor a wedding consultant can save you. Most couples work these days, as do their parents and even grandparents. You may not have the time to plan the wedding the way you'd like, nor people in your circle of family and friends who can help you.

What about Experience?

Ask your prospective wedding consultant about her experience. Some people take special courses; others use the term loosely to describe themselves when they only want to sell you their very own goods or services. Depending on the amount of work you'll have the consultant do for you, you may not need someone with professional training, so be clear on what services you actually need.

 *Essential*

Some wedding consultants have completed training and certification to become certified wedding consultants. Information on what to look for if you're interested in hiring a wedding consultant is on the Association of Certified Professional Wedding Consultants Web site, *www.acpwc.com*.

Some wedding consultants provide rental items for a wedding and reception, such as candleholders, chairs, and vases. Do some comparison shopping to price these items in advance so you know you're not being overcharged.

Whether you choose a wedding consultant or a "wedding services provider," be sure you get a list of references and call them. Talk to former clients and find out, first, whether the consultant did all she was supposed to do. Also, take the time to get a feel for the wedding consultant so you can determine whether she will provide the style and quality of service you want.

Always remember to fully examine the claims of any wedding consultant. Ask your friends for the names of consultants they can recommend. Call the Better Business Bureau in your area to determine whether any complaints have been filed against any person or business you will be working with for your wedding and reception.

Questions for a Wedding Consultant

If you choose to hire a wedding consultant, here are a few questions to ask:

1. How many weddings in this area have you helped plan?

2. What can you do in terms of the style of wedding we are planning on?

3. Can you offer any discounts with vendors you have partnerships with?

4. What exactly do your services cover? What packages do you offer?

5. What are your payment and cancellation policies?

6. What special talents or experience do you have that might help in planning our wedding?

7. How many weddings do you plan at once, and will you be able to be there on our wedding day? (Look for wedding consultants who plan two or three weddings a month. Any more than that and chances are your wedding won't get the attention it deserves.)

The answers to these questions will give you an idea of the caliber of wedding consultant you are dealing with and whether you can work comfortably with her.

Going Solo

If you don't hire a wedding consultant, remember that reception sites such as hotels also have event planners who can help a good deal in planning your wedding and reception. They know their sites inside and out, and they can be invaluable in deciding on the timing of every last detail.

Thinking Outside the Box

In preparation for your wedding, bear in mind that many services offered don't have set prices and are open for discussion. If you've never bargained with a salesperson or vendor, now is the time to learn that negotiating is an acceptable practice and can be beneficial for all involved.

Often, vendors would rather compromise on a price than lose the sale.

How you approach a vendor can result in successful savings on options. For example, you could offer to have a friend pick up the cake to save on a delivery fee, if that's possible.

 Fact

There's a fine line between a simple mention and running a tacky ad, so try not to cross it. If you decide on such an exchange, including a personal thank-you to certain vendors on the back of your program is subtle yet effective. A full-page spread that announces the name of your wedding-gown designer isn't.

A Novel Idea

Recently, some couples have arranged to list their vendors' names on the back of their wedding programs in exchange for free goods, services, or a concession in price. They pay next to nothing for their wedding day in exchange for advertising.

Protect Yourself

Remember to get every business transaction in writing. This cannot be stressed enough. You don't want to have to put down additional deposits when you find that your arrangements have fallen through. Too much is at stake to rely on verbal assurances.

Putting big purchases on a credit card is also worthwhile. First and foremost, you will have more consumer recourse if something goes wrong than if you pay with a check. Second, you may also reap the benefits of points, air miles, or other promotional programs. Your honeymoon is the perfect opportunity to take advantage of such perks, so call your credit card company and see what they have available. Be sure to read the terms and conditions thoroughly. To take full advantage of this money-saving technique, you absolutely must pay the card's balance in full each month.

 Essential

The summer months—June through August—are the most popular for weddings. Beware of other high-traffic dates, such as Valentine's Day and New Year's Eve. Be sensitive to your guests' schedules, and take into account religious holidays, big sporting events, and school holidays.

Flexible Scheduling

You may be able to save a significant amount of money if you have the flexibility to schedule your wedding (or even just the honeymoon) during the off-peak season. Vendors may be willing to negotiate with you for lower fees. You will also enjoy less crowded conditions at wedding and honeymoon venues.

As you plan your date, ask yourselves how important the month and even the day of the week is to you. If you are having a small wedding and most of your guests are local, a Friday evening or Sunday afternoon wedding could work well. As long as you are within your budget, what you save on one area of expense can be put toward another.

Get Online

Logging on to the Internet can be the single biggest money and time saver of all. There are thousands of wedding Web sites with advice and suggestions, ranging from those of professional bridal magazines to recently married couples eager to share with other couples what worked and what didn't.

Use search engines to find wedding locations in the area you're considering. Skimming through the listed sites can make selecting locations a breeze—you can usually view the facilities and eliminate many options that way.

 Question?

How can the Internet make planning a wedding easier?
You'll spend less time surfing the Internet than you would chasing all over town. Use the Internet to buy goods and services or just to investigate what's out there for your wedding and how much it might cost.

You will also find many Web sites maintained by wedding location specialists, from private entrepreneurs to local and state agencies in charge of parks and civic sites. You'll save the time and money required to drive all over or make phone calls, and you'll also save personal energy. Sites such as eBay are increasingly popular for finding bargains, including wedding dresses, veils, wedding party clothes, tuxedos, and accessories.

E-Mail, not Snail Mail

You probably use e-mail to correspond with friends and family. Now you can save a lot of hassle by using e-mail rather than postal mail to let them know about your wedding plans and share photos of dresses and locations. Use them as a support group and get immediate feedback, share interesting Web sites, and compare photos.

Preliminary Time Budget Worksheet

Many people will tell you to begin planning your wedding a year in advance. If your time frame is a shorter one, don't panic. Just advance steps as you need to, delegate, and set your priorities from the start.

To Do	Date Done	Deposit	Final Payment
Set the date			
Decide on number of guests			
Set budget			
Reserve ceremony site			
Reserve reception site			
Hire wedding consultant			
Arrange for a wedding officiant			
Plan the engagement party			
Order wedding and other invitations			
Mail wedding and other invitations			
Order or buy wedding dress and accessories			
Order or buy tuxedos and accessories			

Order or buy bridesmaids' dresses			
Take care of dress alterations			
Put deposit down on flowers			
Put deposit down on cake			
Put deposit down on catering			
Put deposit down on music			
Put deposit down on transportation			
Put deposit down on photographer			
Put deposit down on videographer			
Put deposit down on rental items			
Get blood tests and marriage license			
Make hair and makeup appointment			
Buy wedding rings			

Buy/make wedding favors			
Buy attendants' gifts			
Plan rehearsal dinner			
Plan other functions, such as brunch			
Plan honeymoon			
Make reservations and travel plans			
Get wedding insurance			
Get travel insurance			

Chapter 3
The Wedding Ceremony

This is it—time to plan where to have your wedding ceremony! Maybe you or your fiancé already know where you want to get married. Perhaps it's someplace you have dreamed about for a long time. Here's hoping that you haven't, though, because it can be such fun to look for that special place. There are some wonderful ways to find the place you want for the price you want.

Your Vision for Your Day

First make a date with your fiancé to sit down and talk about where to have your ceremony. Set aside a few hours and together list some of the possible places for a wedding. Perhaps there are some you haven't thought of, and this time together can inspire you to consider them as potential candidates for the perfect wedding site.

Try not to rule anything out at first. Sometimes a location that's not a church or synagogue that seems expensive at certain times of the year—especially a destination wedding location—may be affordable during the off-season. There may be upgrades and amenities available if you persist in thoroughly investigating a promising location. Maybe the setting sounds good to one of you but not the other. At least do some research, consider the possibility, talk about it, then decide.

The Ceremony Site Starts It All

The ceremony site will dictate everything else about the wedding—attire, reception possibilities, transportation requirements, decorations—so it makes sense to start planning the wedding here.

Some couples want to have both the wedding and the reception in the same place. They don't want a big gap in their day, especially if time spent taking photographs after the wedding will slow the celebration down. Then again, the location may simply lend itself to having both ceremony and reception there.

Alert

If you're stressed about all the decisions you have to make and how much money the wedding will cost you, remember that in the end what matters is how happy you and your fiancé are that day—not that every last detail of the ceremony and reception is perfect.

If, however, you want to be married in a religious ceremony in a church, synagogue, or other place of worship, it's fine to have the reception elsewhere. Sometimes a church or synagogue doesn't have a reception hall or can't accommodate your needs.

What's Most Important?

By this point in your life, you've probably attended several weddings and observed (even critiqued) even more on television and at the movies. You've formed an idea of what's important to you. Regardless of whether you have a modest or a luxurious budget, it's very important to incorporate your priorities. If you have your heart set on a seaside location, don't rule it out because you live in a landlocked area. Rethink your options and be creative. If you can't travel to the water, maybe a gorgeous park with a fountain will work just as well.

So Many Ideas!

Locations for ceremony sites are almost limitless. Picture your wedding in each location you and your fiancé consider, then make appointments to visit your final choices.

Religious Weddings

Many couples choose to have a traditional ceremony in a place of worship. Sometimes they're an active member or frequent attendee, and they can't think of any place more appropriate. Other couples, who don't necessarily consider themselves religious, still want to be married in a religious setting. Perhaps such a site is traditional in your family, and you find yourself looking for a place of religious significance for your wedding day.

However, a wedding ceremony can be just as spiritual in a nontraditional setting. Once you start looking at alternative places for your ceremony, you may find that the savings over a formal church or synagogue wedding can be significant in some cases.

 Fact

"We wanted to get married in my church, but were surprised by how expensive it was going to be," said one bride. "It's a large church, and its usage fee is based on that. But we will be inviting only a hundred guests, and we have a limited budget."

Taking It Outside

Upon discovering that a church wedding would blow their budget, one couple looked into having a ceremony in a different location. An outdoor location appealed to the groom-to-be, so one afternoon he surprised his fiancée with a picnic lunch and a list of sites he thought would be perfect. They looked them over, and then ate lunch in a little park beside a beautiful river—the place he secretly liked best but wanted to see her reaction to. She loved it, and her minister was happy to marry the couple there.

Of course, outdoor locations abound. There are beautiful parks located in nearly every community, many with pavilions, gazebos, or other special structures that make for a truly lovely ceremony. If you live near the ocean, you can get married on the beach at daybreak or sunset. There's nothing quite like standing near a vast, serene blue sea for a backdrop to a new life together.

Outdoor locations can be less expensive than a church or synagogue setting, but can be problematic. Consider the following questions: Do you have a backup plan if the weather is bad? Is the terrain easy to walk on, especially for women in high heels or any guests who may be disabled? What kind of permits do you have to get from local authorities, and how expensive are they? Will you need to rent outdoor restroom facilities?

One couple met while performing in an outdoor theater production in California. "We were both so passionate about acting, about being part of the troupe which was just like a family," said Tiffany. "We wanted them to be part of our wedding, so it just seemed natural to have the wedding on the stage after the last performance. Everyone had such a great time and a nice side benefit was that we saved a lot of money."

Some couples meet while attending college, and so getting married in the college chapel or outdoors in a special spot where they met or studied together can be memorable. More and more couples are finding that getting married there feels "just right," and is the fitting transition to a new life together. Is there some special place that has meaning for you and your fiancé? Why not make it a part of your wedding day? Keep an eye out for ceremony sites that can double as reception sites.

Country Clubs

Country clubs are ideal for weddings. Ceremonies can take place outdoors on or near a golf course or indoors in the clubhouse. Receptions can also be held on-site, and you can rent golf carts as convenient transportation for you and your guests. Country clubs with spas often offer special pampering packages for the bride and her attendants. Some country clubs require that you be a member to be married on their premises, but this is not always essential.

Perhaps a country club is out of reach, but there are ample alternatives. Look into private clubhouses that are owned by neighborhood associations in upscale residential developments. Cities have waterfront civic buildings that can be ideal. Check the Yellow Pages and newspaper bridal sections for locations that can provide a country club atmosphere for much less money.

Make Your Own History

Historic mansions or plantations can be elegant sites; they are often so beautifully furnished and landscaped that they require little decoration for the ceremony. Such a location lends itself to photogenic backdrops for your wedding album. Check out stately historical homes in your area. There may be a historic inn, lighthouse, or pier that would make a unique setting for your wedding.

Make Your Own Art

Museums and cultural centers make lovely sites for weddings with their displays of artwork and elegant settings. Casual wedding sites include parks, country farms, even country and western clubs where you, your new spouse, and your guests can do the two-step after the ceremony.

 Fact

Individuals other than ministers or rabbis can officiate at your wedding. Your county courthouse has information on how to become an officiant for a specific date or event. Even if you don't save money over the cost of hiring a member of the clergy, the honor of having a friend or family member marry you is priceless.

Visit prospective locations together. If you find a location you like, stay there for a while to see whether you feel the kind of mood you want for your wedding. Factor in noise level, likely temperatures, and acoustics.

Questions for Ceremony Site Coordination

Here are some important questions to ask the coordinator of each ceremony site you visit:

1. What dates are available?

2. What is the fee? Does the fee change depending on the requested time of day or day of the week? When do we need to put down our deposit?

3. What are the seating options? Do we need to rent chairs and other items for the ceremony?

4. How long can we have the site? Does the ceremony need to end by a certain time?

5. When can our florist arrive to decorate? Who will be here early to open the facility?

6. Are there any restrictions on decorating?

7. Is there an attached reception hall in case we decide to use it? What is the fee? What are the cleaning costs?

8. Can we bring in our own caterer if we want? What about alcohol?

9. For an outdoor location: Where can we move the wedding if it rains?

10. Is there a place for members of the wedding party to get dressed?

In evaluating a site's conditions, be clear about your mutual priorities and be aware of what features you're willing to compromise on. You don't want to end up booking a facility that doesn't meet your most important needs.

No Place Like Home?

Private homes, which have long been used for weddings, are becoming more popular with couples who want a smaller, more intimate wedding with fewer guests. Whether your home is large or small, a wedding held there can make you and your partner feel comfortable and cherished.

Savings Begin at Home

Savings can be considerable when the ceremony is held at home. You don't have to budget for the usage or rental fee of a church or synagogue, and there's no institutional cleaning fee or transportation expenses. Decorations can be kept to a minimum, since your home is already furnished.

Childhood Dreams

"I dreamed of walking down our staircase to meet my husband-to-be from the first time I saw my family home as a little girl," a friend once confided. "I used to practice walking down the steps, holding a feather duster and pretending it was my bouquet. My mom and dad were thrilled when I asked if my fiancé and I could be married there. We stood before the fireplace and exchanged vows."

Ceremonies at home can also take place around a sparkling swimming pool or in a corner of a lovely garden. Even the plainest garden can be inexpensively adorned with candles and pots of flowers from a discount florist or local nursery.

It Doesn't Have to Be Your Home

If a friend has a house you really love, consider asking him whether you can be married there. Most people feel flattered by such a request. New bride Olivia estimated that she saved $400 on ceremony expenses and had a wedding that was particularly special because she decided to have a home wedding.

"A friend of mine had a big Victorian home that she knew I just loved," she said. "When I asked if Mark and I could be married there, she cried. We planted some flowers for the backyard ceremony and she said that now when she looks at them she remembers that day, and she's happy."

Olivia figures she saved an additional $500 because she automatically limited her guest list due to the smaller size of the house. She didn't have to order expensive floral decorations for the church and reception site either. Much of the catering was also assembled at home.

 Alert

If you decide to have a home wedding, don't waste your savings by buying new furniture or drapes. The guests won't be focusing on your home since they'll be too busy looking at the bride and groom.

Three Weddings, Three Budgets

Susan and Nick were sitting together at their favorite spot on campus one day in between classes, talking about where they wanted to get married.

"It was so peaceful there. The alumni association gave the college money to make this big reflecting pool, and flowers were blooming and a little family of ducks was out on the water. We just looked at each other and thought, how perfect! We should get married here! After all, college is where we met, dated, shared so many special memories. What could be better?"

They investigated and found out that other students and alumni had had the same idea. "But we managed to get the date we wanted, and as soon-to-be graduates, we were entitled to the alumni rate. It was a huge savings from other ceremony sites."

Tradition, Tradition

Kylie and Sean have decided on a traditional church wedding. "There was some initial family discussion about which church. Our family is Methodist, Sean's is Presbyterian. In the end, maybe because my parents were paying, Sean's family told us we should get married in my family's church."

Because they wanted to show their appreciation for a peaceful resolution to what they had feared would be a tense situation, Kylie and Sean decided to look for a reception site that would honor Sean's parents.

Help Us Celebrate!

Lynn and John didn't find themselves agreeing quickly on their wedding site. "We knew we wanted to have a big party, and it didn't seem quite right to have that in a church reception hall. Then, too, we aren't members of a church, so we didn't think we wanted to ask if we could get married in one and never go back."

A discussion with her wedding planner resulted in a perfect location for the couple, according to Lynn. "I liked the idea of a country club and John liked a location with water. The planner told us about a marina country club and made arrangements for us to visit it. We decided it was perfect." Lynn's location is pricey, but with alteration such a setting can be affordable for couples on a modest or moderate budget.

Destination Weddings to Fit Your Budget

For some couples, there's nothing better than a destination wedding, which can provide the opportunity to gather friends and family before the wedding for a festive time. A side benefit, of course, is that the location can double as a honeymoon destination. Sometimes couples reason that they are saving money by combining the sites. Others feel that even though the expense can be high, the beauty of a ceremony and honeymoon in an exotic and romantic setting is worth the extra cash.

A destination wedding can be held anywhere in the world, including on any of the oceans. Cruise ships offer wedding packages, and you can choose any number of exotic locations in the world for a wedding. But you don't need to get carried away. A nice beach ceremony a few states away could satisfy you.

Is It Worth the Challenge?

There can be a number of challenges to planning a destination wedding. You might have to deal with unfamiliar regulations, work with vendors you don't know, and have fewer guests at the wedding because of the expense. This final point can be seen as either a negative or a positive, depending on how you feel about having certain family members at your wedding! All joking aside, destination weddings require significant planning.

Destination Locations

Disney World in Orlando, Florida, offers a variety of wedding services in their many themed hotels, with the bonus of fun and adventurous honeymoon options right there in the theme parks. It's a stateside destination location that may also appeal to your guests, particularly if children will be attending.

Riverboats that traverse the Mississippi or a river near you are also hot spots for weddings. Couples can choose to reserve an entire cruise or just a portion of it. A special plus: The captain can perform the ceremony.

 Fact

Marriages of U.S. citizens in foreign countries are recognized legally in this country. Consult with officials in the country you want to be married in for requirements well ahead of the date you want to be married.

Look for deals online by typing your requirements into a search engine such as Yahoo! or Google. Try simple phrases such as "wedding packages under $500." One couple found a Lake Tahoe location that offers several packages starting with a simple economy wedding for $275, which includes obtaining, filing, and notarizing the marriage license. Upgrading with more elaborate flowers, more chapel time, videography, and additional features increases the price, of course. The most expensive package tops out at several thousand dollars and includes a three-hour stretch limousine rental.

Essential

Bed-and-breakfasts, inns, vineyards, and similar settings offer opportunities for elegant wedding ceremonies at varying prices. Some vineyards specialize in wine-pairing meals; others can provide lodging for you and your guests. Check out the prices for these types of sites in your desired location.

If either of you has interests such as Renaissance fairs or historical re-enactments, you may want to get married in period costumes. Do some research to see if you can get married at these sites for a little expense. Imagine the effect of having your marriage ceremony conducted by someone dressed as a king or a military captain. Again, items such as flowers and other decorations can be downplayed not only for savings, but also because they wouldn't be historically accurate.

Destination Logistics

Be ready to do a lot of research or consult a travel agent on traveling in your chosen area. Don't give up until you're happy with your choice.

Even if you choose a destination resort that does most of the wedding planning for you, you still have to make decisions about:

- Flowers
- Music
- Photography
- Ceremony readings and vows
- Reception food and drink
- Ceremony and reception music
- Wedding cake
- Wedding attire

Don't be overwhelmed by this list! Even if you have never been to the destination, there are ways to find reputable vendors to work with.

Ask the Destination Site for Help

It's possible to save money, time, and trouble by asking managers of your chosen site whether a wedding or event consultant is available to help you arrange a wedding. Most of the time there is. Be sure to ask whether there is any fee for such services. Most destinations are eager for your business and usually provide wedding services at no extra charge.

Questions about the Destination

The best part of a destination wedding is using the location's natural elements—the beautiful natural setting of Hawaii, for instance, inspires a special mood for a wedding ceremony. Perhaps that is why it was one of the first destination wedding/honeymoon locations, and to this day remains a premier site. What is it about your potential destination site that inspires you to say your vows there?

Alert

There are dozens of Web sites about destination weddings on the Internet. You can find out about the most popular wedding destinations, check out some bargains, and even chat online with other couples who have chosen to have a destination wedding and are willing to share their experiences.

Ten important considerations if planning a destination wedding:

1. Can your family and wedding party travel to the site?

2. Who will pay for their airfare and accommodations?

3. What types of arrangements are available for on-site weddings?

4. Can you get an upgrade on your accommodations by having your wedding at the same site?

5. How many rooms can the site provide for your guests?

6. Will you be able to secure a special rate for accommodations? (Check with the airlines, too.)

7. When do you have to make a deposit and how much must it be?

8. Ask to see sample menus and photos of actual weddings that have taken place at the destination.

9. Are there any special weather considerations?

10. Is there a one-year anniversary return special for having a wedding there?

Ceremony and Reception Time Budget Worksheet for Planning the Ceremony and Reception

Many people will tell you to begin planning your wedding a year in advance. If that time frame will be shorter for you, don't panic! Just move the steps up as you need to, delegate, and set your priorities from the start!

To Do	Date Done	Deposit Made	Final Payment Made
Set the date			
Decide on number of guests			
Set budget			
Reserve ceremony site			
Reserve reception site			
Hire wedding consultant (if desired)			
Arrange for a wedding officiant			
Order wedding and other invitations			

Mail wedding and other invitations			
Order or buy wedding dress and accessories			
Order or buy tuxedos and accessories			
Order or buy bridesmaids' dresses			
Take care of dress alterations			
Put deposit down on flowers			
Put deposit down on cake			
Put deposit down on catering			
Put deposit down on music			
Put deposit down on transportation			
Put deposit down on photographer			
Put deposit down on videographer			
Put deposit down on rental items			

Get blood tests and marriage license			
Make hair and makeup appointment			
Buy wedding rings			
Buy/make wedding favors			
Buy wedding-party gifts and other gifts			
Plan the engagement party			
Plan rehearsal dinner			
Plan other functions, such as brunch			
Plan honeymoon			
Make reservations and travel plans			
Get wedding insurance			
Get travel insurance			
Schedule a break for bride and groom before ceremony			

Chapter 4
The Reception Site

For the vast majority of nuptial celebrations, the reception is the most costly part of the budget. Couples enthusiastically plan a terrific party for their friends and family to celebrate their marriage. Then, suddenly, they're in over their heads and spending too much money! This chapter will help you avoid potential monetary pitfalls as you plan your reception.

The Big Day, Act Two

Many people get caught up in the emotion and excitement of planning a wedding and start adding extras left and right. Whether it's last-minute invitees or extra touches that you've realized you must have, the figure originally budgeted is suddenly a distant memory. Often adding a single expense causes other expenses to mushroom until finally—pow!—there goes the budget.

 Alert

If your guest list is getting out of hand, put the brakes on it, quick. Separate your guests into two categories, A and B. The A list contains your mother and other guests who absolutely must attend. The B list contains your mother's coworker and guests who would simply be nice to invite.

It doesn't have to be that way. Take a deep breath and remember what's important here. Your wedding day is all about celebrating your special day with the people you care about and who care about you.

When it really comes down to it, no one wants to see you bankrupt or stressed because of the wedding or the reception. Even if you have a luxurious budget, you still want to spend your money wisely.

Your Options Are Diverse

Your options are defined by two basic factors: the size of your guest list and your budget. Local bridal magazines and wedding Web sites like The Knot (*www.theknot.com*)

carry information on typical reception venues in your area, but they only cover a fraction of what's available.

 Fact

The chamber of commerce, private estates, and historical societies often have buildings that are available for weddings or receptions.

Sallie chose a civic center whose museum-like gallery was the perfect site for her winter wedding. Sallie and her bridesmaids turned the gallery into a fairy-tale setting of silk ficus topiary trees strung with twinkling lights and wrapped with tulle. When the lights were dimmed and candles were set in rented candelabra on the tables, the gallery became a truly magical setting. The beautiful artwork on the walls contributed to the elegance of the room, and the nearby kitchen was convenient for the caterer.

Country clubs, marinas, museums, private estates, fellowship halls, and art centers are good reception sites. One couple had their reception in the private lounge of the oceanside restaurant where they'd had their first date. In a lounge just big enough for the family and half a dozen wedding guests, they had a great time.

Consider having a reception at home—your home or someone else's. Perhaps a friend or family member has a house with a lovely garden patio or a pool where a reception could be held. Be considerate if one of your loved ones agrees to host your reception. Preparations and cleanup for the big day can be disruptive, so make sure the host is truly willing to make this sacrifice.

 Fact

You might think you know your area, but chances are you may not have heard of a dream reception site right around the corner from your ceremony site. Check with your local chamber of commerce or research local or state Web sites and travel bureaus.

For above-average budgets, Disney offers fairy-tale wedding packages at their resorts and on cruises. Some all-inclusive packages will take care of little details for you. Other theme parks and attractions also host wedding couples.

Location Is Everything

Decide how close you want the reception to be to the ceremony. Visit at least two places that each of you thinks would make a good reception location. The idea is to stay flexible in your thinking, and to brainstorm. Sometimes the planning for a wedding becomes so intense that you just want to make quick decisions, pay the money, and settle matters. Getting it settled, however, should not mean settling!

Church Reception Halls

Perhaps your fiancé likes the idea of having the reception in the hall attached to your church or synagogue.

Nearly one out of four couples who marry in a church have their reception in the church hall, often because the bride or the groom, or both, are members of the church and it makes sense to stay there after the ceremony. There's a sense of rightness to the place that makes you want to continue your celebration there.

There's no question that it's very convenient to have the reception at your place of worship following the ceremony. Guests can move easily into adjoining reception space while you have your wedding pictures taken, and you don't have to worry about your octogenarian relatives navigating busy highways. Weather is another factor. For instance, if you're having a winter wedding in a cold climate, staying inside in one location is a bonus.

 Essential

Check with the church regarding its rules about using the hall, particularly about any restrictions on serving alcoholic drinks and dancing. It may also have rules about hours for hall rental and how you may decorate the place.

Because you already have an established relationship with the facility, you have a reduced risk of complications, conflicts, and potential crises. That's not to say you shouldn't be just as diligent about setting expectations and getting the details in writing, but you can find some peace of mind in knowing that you're familiar with your venue.

Convenience and price breaks are fine reasons to remain at your church or synagogue. Add to that the fact that most reception halls are well maintained and often decorated, and you have quite a plus.

It's an Important Day—Choose Carefully

Alternatively, perhaps you've always wanted to have a reception in an elegant place like a hotel. Maybe a flower-filled garden setting seems perfect for your reception, or perhaps you know of a beautiful riverside park.

Whatever it is, set aside a few hours to visit the locations together. Really look them over and talk about the vision each of you has for the reception. Think about the kind of celebration both you and your guests could have there. You'll always remember the place where you celebrate your wedding, so make it a place that is truly special to you.

Open-Air Receptions

Susan and Nick talked about where they'd have their reception right after they decided to hold the wedding ceremony by the reflecting pool on the campus of their college.

"We looked at a few places, like the fancy reception rooms they have for functions for special guests on campus," Susan said. "We also checked out some other places like meeting rooms at restaurants and places like that."

Alert

Depending on your location and the season, an outdoor reception might be an option. If you decide on one, have a backup plan in case of bad weather. Look into tent rentals to shield guests from sun and showers.

Susan and Nick gave a little more thought to their vision. "We got to talking about how nice it was going to be to be outside in the sunshine after all that time in class-rooms, and we had that harpist . . . well, it just seemed natural to stay there and have a picnic with the two dozen or so people we invited."

Other Money-Saving Facilities

Since Kylie's mother is a member of the Women's Club, Kylie and Sean decided the club's facility was a perfect choice. Each year, the club hosts many weddings for children of members and others from the community.

"The catering would be a bit steeper than we planned, but still much less than a hotel reception," Kylie said. "My dad offered to give us money to elope instead of having a wedding and reception! We think he was joking."

Actually, because her mother is a member, there was a discount for renting the facility. "We compared the prices for a luncheon reception and a sit-down dinner, and we saved by choosing the luncheon—a buffet, actually."

Private clubs such as the Women's Club or fraternal clubs offer many benefits to their members and to the community. Such places can accommodate all kinds of events and usually have everything you need—the space, the furnishings, kitchen facilities, parking, and sometimes even security.

Question?

What resources can reception sites provide?
Often, the person in charge of renting out a private club can also recommend caterers, florists, and musicians who have done a good job for other events held there. Coordinators often keep albums of events held there, which can offer a wealth of decorating ideas, too.

All about the Party

Lynn and John plan to spend the largest portion of their wedding budget on the reception, so finding the perfect place was very important to them.

"We'll have the wedding outside on a small pavilion overlooking the water at the marina country club; then we'll move inside to a sit-down dinner and later, a dance," Lynn explained. "My list of 'have-to-haves' is simple: We have to have a place that serves champagne and drinks and has a dance floor and space for the jazz group we want."

Although they want to have a big party for their family and friends to celebrate their wedding, Lynn and John also know they don't want it to go on too long. "We've both been to receptions that went on for so long that people had too much to drink, and it wasn't pleasant," said John. "So prearranging a time for things to be over before Lynn and I leave for the airport for Hawaii is important."

Learning What to Look For

Make a list of the qualities you're looking for in a reception site and prioritize them. Some are non-negotiable; if a site doesn't have space for all your guests, it won't do. Some characteristics can be more adaptable. For example, you can make any place more romantic or cheerful with the right decorations.

Time Is Money

The day of the week and time of day you hold your reception directly affects the cost. If you plan your reception for midafternoon, guests won't expect a big sit-down meal. Picking up the bar tab can be expensive, but you can save money by offering only certain drinks or having the reception in the morning or early afternoon.

Caterers and reception sites often charge a premium for Saturday night weddings. Scheduling your wedding at any other time can mean big savings for you. No matter the budget you are using—modest, moderate, or luxurious— you can control spending by giving some thought to timing and scheduling during the early stages of planning.

Look It Over

Visit your prospective reception site and pay attention to the details. Walk through the interior and note the table linens and silverware, watch how the wait staff take care of patrons, and check out the restrooms and other amenities.

Most public places and businesses are in compliance with federal disability guidelines, but if you have anyone in your wedding party who would find it a difficult place to gain access to, you might rethink the site.

 Essential

The time also sets the mood for your wedding. The expectations guests have for refreshments and entertainment at a Saturday night event are different than that for a Sunday afternoon gathering, when you can offer something simpler and less expensive.

What about Food?

Some reception sites have their own caterers, but other sites require you to find your own. Some places will let you bring in your own caterer, but will charge a fee for not using their services. You may prefer the convenience of an all-in-one package over the responsibility of locating a reliable caterer. Be sure you get information for a variety of scenarios as you do your research.

The answers to questions about food can significantly affect your decision, and certainly affect your budget. Be mindful of time, money, and energy—and of your priorities—as you make your decision.

Let the Reception Site Coordinator Help You

When you visit your reception sites, take the opportunity to ask the coordinator some important questions:

1. What is the rental charge for the dates and times? What are the rates for other dates and times?

2. How many hours does the fee include?

3. What is the seating capacity for the room?

4. What is included in the price?

5. Are parking and valet service included?

6. What is the cancellation policy?

7. Is catering provided or can/must we arrange it ourselves?

8. If we choose to arrange the catering ourselves, is there a fee attached?

9. Is alcohol provided or may we bring our own? If we supply our own, are there corkage or other

fees? Can we arrange an open bar, and what are the rates for that?

10. If we'd like to bring a band/deejay/ensemble, is there a place for them to set up, and is there any charge for this?

11. Is there a cleanup fee, or is cleanup included in the price?

12. Can we rent other necessities such as tableware, linens, candleholders, and so on? What are the setup and/or cleanup fees associated with additional services?

Ask the coordinators for pictures of events that have been held at the reception site. Ask for references—and check them out—to minimize any chance you'll encounter problems. Many sites will also offer you a taste test of the food you'll be served. If they don't, ask for it.

No Surprises!

Lynn and John knew that they wouldn't need to ask for a taste of the food because they'd been to the marina country club for dinner. But when they made the formal arrangements, the club's coordinator still made sure they had a tour of the place and spent time reviewing the details, making sure they'd have the reception they wanted.

If you have other questions, now is the time to ask them, before you put down your deposit. Remember to use a credit card in case you have problems later.

The Deposit's Down—Now What?

Congratulations! You've made two of the biggest decisions! It's time to take a deep breath and relax a little and have fun with the rest of the wedding details. Just think of the decisions you've already made, the research you've done, and all the discussing and compromising you've gone through. You've done so much.

If you've brought in your expenses under budget so far, good for you! If not, then the remainder of this book is especially important for helping you have the wedding you want within the budget you've set.

Reception Budget Worksheet

Use this handy worksheet to document expenses for your reception. Keeping track of everything you spend will ensure that you stay within your budget. You might want to make a copy of the worksheet and tuck it into your purse or daily calendar so you remember to make entries as soon as you make the purchases. You might need to customize this worksheet a bit, depending on your particular reception plans.

Rental of hall or
reception site: $_____
Food: $_____

Beverages:	$_____
Wedding cake:	$_____
Cake knife, cake stand, and other utensils:	$_____
Music:	$_____
Decorations:	$_____
Chair rental:	$_____
Miscellaneous:	$_____

Other Expenses:

_____	$_____
_____	$_____
_____	$_____

Total: $_____

Time Budget Worksheet

Many people will tell you to begin planning your wedding a year in advance. If that time frame will be shorter for you, don't panic! Just move the steps up as you need to, delegate, and set your priorities from the start!

To Do	Date Done/Deposit Made/ Final Payment Made
Reserve reception site:	_____
Put deposit down on catering:	_____
Miscellaneous details:	_____
Miscellaneous details:	_____
Miscellaneous details:	_____

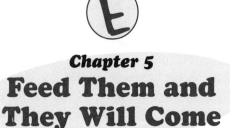

Chapter 5
Feed Them and They Will Come

After you've chosen your reception site, consider what you want to serve your guests. Reception food often becomes a subject of debate for wedding planners, but don't despair. You don't need to overextend your budget to have a great reception. Wedding cakes no longer are featured exclusively in the wedding dessert market. Explore the options that are right for you and your budget. This chapter shows you how to pick the best food and beverages for your particular wedding reception.

How Much Can You Expect to Pay?

Reception food is usually calculated on a per-person basis. For instance, let's say you want to invite 200 people for a sit-down dinner, and the least expensive individual meal you can get at your reception site is $30. Simple math quickly shows this will cost you $6,000. But what if you don't want to spend that much on reception food? You have two options: You can either keep the number of guests to a minimum, or you can avoid a sit-down dinner and save on the per-person fee.

Beyond Sit-Down Dinners

The time of day you get married determines what kind of meal you should serve your guests. In basic terms, the earlier in the day you get married, the less expensive the meal choices are. Reception food for a dinner will cost more than a luncheon or a breakfast. Get married at sunrise, and you can have an elegant wedding breakfast or brunch. You'll save a lot of money and have a truly unique wedding event.

If you want to hold a dinner event, set up a buffet or dinner stations. Guests can serve themselves, and you won't have to pay for extra wait staff. Letting guests select what they like also keeps wasted food to a minimum (some adults still won't eat vegetables!). Dinner stations are becoming increasingly popular at weddings. Stations can include entrées, vegetable side dishes, breads, and desserts.

Weddings and receptions that begin at midday or later tend to be more popular and better attended. That means more of your invited guests will show up; you need to take that into consideration for your head count.

Luncheon or tea menus cost a bit more than breakfast menus, but they're less expensive than a sit-down dinner. And dinnertime receptions pose another problem—whether you should serve alcoholic beverages and, if so, whether these should be "on the house" or sold at a cash bar. Offering your guests an unlimited (or open) bar will hike up your reception cost to an extreme.

Money-Saving Menus

A suggestion for a simple breakfast or brunch menu in the modest budget category could consist of scrambled eggs, bacon or sausage, potatoes, fruit, sweet rolls, coffee, tea, and juice. This general menu can be adapted for a moderate budget. Offer omelets with several fillings, two breakfast meats, home fries or grits, an assortment of breakfast pastries, coffee, tea, hot chocolate, and several juices.

A luxurious wedding breakfast or brunch includes eggs Benedict or a similar egg specialty, crêpes or Belgian waffles, spiral-sliced ham or shrimp cocktail, fruit compote, flavored coffees or cappuccinos, teas, several juice selections, and mimosas (champagne and orange juice cocktails). Or plan an elegant lunch of a chicken or fish dish with a few elegantly prepared vegetable dishes. These menus will cost less than the meat menus often served at dinner receptions. Chicken can range from simple, inexpensive dishes up to coq au vin. Seafood can be broiled with a light sauce for a modest or moderate budget; luxurious budgets can splurge on lobster. Your caterer can make suggestions based on your budget.

Let's say you've decided on an early morning wedding. Don't think it needs to be a sit-down occasion. If you want to save money, you can offer a table set with breakfast pastries, coffee, tea, and juices. If you are working with a moderate budget, you could feature a buffet table with your menu choices.

Avoid a Meal Altogether

Some couples are skipping wedding meals by scheduling their reception at nonmeal times, such as in the midafternoon or after dinner. Featuring a selection of hors d'oeuvres or a dessert buffet with appropriate beverages is a very classy option.

Catering Service Savers

If you are having your reception at a hotel or a restaurant, you have to use their services. One of your reasons for choosing that location is presumably because you want to serve their food. If your reception is at a location that does not have food service and you don't want to prepare the food yourself, you will need a caterer.

Question?

How do I find an off-site caterer?

Get a list of caterers from your reception site or from other vendors, such as your wedding coordinator or florist. See whether there's a culinary school or an educational institution in your area that provides catering services; you'll save and also help students launch their careers.

Ask Questions

Don't be intimidated if you've never dealt with a caterer before. Here are some questions to ask to make sure you get what you want for what you want to spend:

1. What can you offer us for our budget?

2. What about substitutions for special diets?

3. Will we need to provide our own dishes, silverware, napkins, and so on? If you provide them, may we see samples?

4. How many servers will there be, and will they do cleanup?

5. Is there a charge to cut the cake? To serve it?

6. What is the deposit schedule?

7. When do you need a final count?

Some reception sites charge the caterer a fee that is added to your bill. Ask both the site and the caterer about their policy on this type of charge.

Cruise Those Menus

Regardless of who provides the food, you can save money by asking a lot of questions and carefully looking over menus so that you receive the most for your budgeted dollars. If either the on-site or the private caterers tend to feature very gourmet entrées, ask whether you can substitute something less expensive.

Being careful with your dollars doesn't mean serving an institutional chicken dinner. Think creatively: Certain herbs, spices, and other fairly simple touches can transform a bird into something quite elegant and less expensive than coq au vin. Even if you want to splurge and have prime rib, not all guests eat beef these days, so you want to provide something different for them anyway. Thinking outside the box with your entrée choices can mean a delicious meal for less money.

When Lynn and John found they'd save money by holding both their ceremony and reception at the marina country club, they could afford to order pricier dishes. Nevertheless, they have kept their fancy reception menu of island favorites relatively simple: seafood salad, fresh lobster, stir-fried vegetables, and ambrosia served in pineapple shells.

After they picked the menu, they were told they could also save by allowing the chef to substitute different seafood and fruit (with their approval) if he hears of a better price or better in-season quality. They quickly agreed.

 Alert

> Take advantage of food tastings. Make an appointment with a caterer to taste some samples of your menu choices. Ask to see photos of the caterer's work, too. Ask for references and follow up on these. And always get everything in writing to prevent misunderstandings.

With a Little Help

You're not really going to have that reception without Aunt Anna's special antipasto platter, are you? Or Grandma Joanna's special-occasion champagne punch? Or your best friend Nancy's incredible cake?

Family inclusion has always been an extremely important part of wedding days. Perhaps some members of your family would like to get more involved in your wedding, and food preparation is a perfect opportunity. You won't know unless you ask. If you ask friends or family members and they seem reluctant, don't push the issue or make them feel guilty. But if they truly want to help, great. This will add such a personal touch to your wedding.

Do You Have Family Favorites?

Even if you have a caterer prepare your food, there may still be some foods and beverages you just can't imagine being fixed by someone other than a particular family member or friend.

Check to make sure you can bring those special food and beverage items to your reception site so they're not wasted or feelings aren't hurt. There should be enough of whatever is brought for most of your guests to have a taste, and the food or beverage should be stored at the proper temperature so there is no food-poisoning issue to ruin the day.

Families Made Their Day

Because Susan and Nick are planning a casual wedding on a very modest budget, they don't want to spend money on an elaborate meal. Even though their college cafeteria does occasionally provide catering services, this option wasn't even discussed because they had eaten the food there for four years.

Susan's aunt has enjoyed preparing elegant box lunches for her garden and community clubs for years, so when she suggested doing so for her niece, Susan jumped at the idea. "It seems perfect to have this kind of food at our outdoor wedding!" Her aunt refused to take any money for supplies from Susan, insisting that this contribution would be her wedding present. It was agreed that Susan's aunt would prepare fancy tea sandwiches, little containers of her renowned pasta and potato salads, and crudités tucked into fancy little white boxes, tied with yellow ribbon, and decorated with sprigs of silk daisies. Iced tea and lemonade would be served as well.

Saving on Champagne and Other Libations

What beverages will you serve at your reception? Time of day plays an important part in determining your best options. Bottles of champagne or other alcoholic beverages aren't freely passed around at a morning wedding reception. A mimosa or maybe a Bloody Mary could be offered at a brunch, but there would be a limit on the number served because of the hour. At luncheons and midafternoon weddings, champagne punch or a glass or two of champagne is appropriate. Again, the time of day dictates that the amount be controlled. During late afternoon or evening weddings, there is no need to control the amount of alcoholic beverages. Rather than serving champagne, some couples choose to serve one drink that reflects the theme of their wedding, like a Mojito for an island wedding.

Don't Let the Dollars Fizz Away

Alcohol can be a huge expense at a reception. Do you want to have a champagne toast? You'll need to check on the alcohol policy at your reception site. Some church reception halls, fraternal halls, and community centers don't permit alcohol at all; many hotels and restaurants want you to buy from them. Is there a charge for corkage or a special bar and bartender arrangement in place?

Essential

If you're not a wine expert, get a friend or a helpful person at the wine shop to guide you in selecting a good vintage with a reasonable price.

Get in writing exactly what you'll be charged for, and make certain the contract includes a stipulation that you'll be consulted if the drink consumption looks as though it will exceed the predetermined dollar amount. A "no-host" or cash bar—one that charges your guests for their drinks—is usually not considered appropriate. You wouldn't invite guests to other functions and expect them to pay for their drinks, so why do it at a wedding?

Beverages on Different Budgets

Susan and Nick can't have alcoholic beverages at their college site, so they'll be toasted with sparkling white grape juice in elegant glasses.

Lynn and John plan on serving champagne and mixed drinks at their reception, but to prevent overimbibing they are establishing a cutoff limit with their bartender. Nonalcoholic drinks for designated drivers and teetotalers will be served, and they've made an arrangement with a taxi company to take home guests who try to leave too inebriated to drive.

Kylie and Sean plan on having one champagne toast, then Grandma Naomi's special champagne punch will be served for the remainder of the reception. "We couldn't imagine a wedding reception or celebration that didn't involve the punch. What's a nice bonus is how it's not only delicious, it's also a money saver over having straight champagne." The punch will be served in an antique punch bowl that's been in the family for years.

The Perfect Wedding Cake on a Budget

How much do you want to budget for your cake? If you have a modest or moderate budget and the cake is not one of the most important elements of your day, something simple like a two- or three-layer cake iced simply and topped with flowers is the least expensive choice.

However, if the cake is a high-priority item for you, consider ordering something more elaborate, such as a multilayered cake with special decoration or one made of multiple layers of various flavors of cheesecake. Choices abound, including cakes filled with fruit, mousse, or fillings made with liqueurs like Amaretto and Grand Marnier. Frostings can be butter cream, Bavarian cream, or whipped cream. Fondant, a mixture of sugar and water cooked to a consistency that can be rolled and molded over a cake, has become very popular because it helps keep a cake fresh and elegant despite the weather.

Alert

First decide what flavor of cake you'd like. If you find that you like a white cake but your fiancé prefers chocolate, you can serve both—it's your cake! Simply ask the baker to do different layers in different flavors.

What Are Your Needs?

When deciding on a cake, consider your needs. How many guests are you inviting? Do you want to save the top layer of your cake to freeze and enjoy on your first anniversary? Will you want a groom's cake as well? Your baker needs to know the answers to these questions in order to tell you how big a cake to order. The size and complexity of the cake, as well as where and when it needs to be delivered, will determine the price.

Top It Off

Once all wedding cakes had to have a bride and groom on the top. Only a few other types of toppers were deemed acceptable. Today it seems like anything goes. Couples are encouraged to try something different and express their imagination. A cake can be decorated with icing patterns that look like lace or fresh flowers and be placed on an antique porcelain cake stand.

Personalize your cake with something that reflects your interests, such as your career, hobbies, or your military experience. Do the two of you like to sky dive or scuba dive? You might want a cake topper to show off this interest. Individuals who make custom cake toppers can make something special that may become a treasured family heirloom. Given a picture or detailed description of a specialty cake, local bakers might be able to duplicate what you have in mind for a lower price.

 Fact

When the estates of the Duke and Duchess of Windsor were sold at auction in 1998, a beribboned box inscribed "A piece of our wedding cake" sold for $26,000 in a very spirited bidding contest. "It's history," said an auction attendee. "He gave up being king of England for his bride."

Beth, a Christmas bride, found a beautiful blown-glass gazebo ornament of a couple embracing inside. The price was right—under $20. Beth's friend Vicki baked a basic round three-layer cake and covered it with a simple white icing, then placed red silk poinsettias, holly, and evergreen around the base of the cake. Vicki hot-glued the bottom of the ornament to a six-inch round mirror and placed this atop the cake. When the light hit the topper, the sparkle was fantastic. It was a bargain, but no one knew.

Today, decorating a wedding cake with fresh flowers rather than a topper is a big trend. Use seasonal flowers to lessen the cost. You can also forgo the cake topper altogether. Some couples feel their cake looks beautiful without one.

 Essential

Resourceful ways to save on your wedding cake include using fake layers to add height but not dollars, serving cakes on pedestals of varying heights instead of offering one big stacked cake, and decorating with flowers instead of relying on lots of fancy frosting details and a cake topper.

Finding the Right Baker

There are so many choices—think of them as opportunities to save! You can find a traditional wedding-cake baker or ask your caterer to bake you a cake. You can order your cake from a grocery store bakery or have a friend or family member make it.

Finding a Special Baker

You'll save your money by going with bakers you've found through references from family and friends. Choosing an unknown baker from the phone book is chancy.

Here are questions to ask a prospective baker:

1. Do you have pictures of cakes you've made for other weddings?

2. If we want something different, can you do a customized cake for us? Do you have any suggestions for one?

3. If we need a cake for a certain number of guests, how much will that cost? (Prices can range from $1 a slice up to $10—or more—depending on your area and how fancy a cake you want.)

4. Will you deliver the cake to our reception site? Is there a delivery charge? A setup charge?

5. How far ahead must we order the cake? How much of a deposit must we put down?

Getting the Most for Your Money

Specifying your order in writing ensures that the cake you pay for is the same one that is delivered to your wedding. Don't order a bigger cake than you need. If you're serving desserts or having a groom's cake, you won't need as many slices. Remember, not everyone who attends necessarily wants a slice of cake.

When a Cake's Not a Cake

One clever bride chose to serve lovely flower-trimmed cupcakes arranged on a tall, tiered pedestal stand. That way each guest could have an individualized serving, which saved on the price of a big cake. The children at the wedding weren't the only ones who were delighted.

The cupcakes were very moist because they were baked in paper wrappings, and the icing details were as decorative as that on a full-sized cake.

 Alert

Be sure the cake won't be delivered too early. This prevents it from being ruined by sitting in a location that is too warm or being jostled by people setting up the reception site. If the reception will be held outdoors, protect the cake from insects. Assign someone to look out for these concerns for you on the day of the wedding.

Small versions of wedding cakes became a trend several years ago and were very popular with wedding bakers because they could charge more for the extra work of creating them. While the little cakes are lovely, you'll have to think about whether you want to budget the amount of money you'll pay for them.

Some couples save by exhibiting a fancy cake for the wedding photos and then serving slices of sheet cake, cut in the kitchen where the guests can't see. Another way to save is to group cake layers of different sizes on acrylic stands, placing the largest at the center front of the cake table.

Bake It Yourself

Don't shy away from letting a friend or family member make your cake. Perhaps one of them has taken a cake decorating class or you've seen her produce wonderful cakes for special occasions. She would most likely welcome the chance to bake your cake as a wedding gift.

Craft stores carry supplies to make wedding and other special-event cakes. There you'll find cake pans, plates, columns, frosting decorations, and toppers—everything you need for a wedding cake.

Fondant for Me

Best of all, you can now find fondant at craft stores. Once available only to professional bakers, fondant is a creamy sugar paste that can be used decoratively in place of traditional frosting. There are even special rolling pins for rolling out the fondant before placing it atop the cake.

Bakers will tell you that fondant covers a multitude of sins, transforming an ordinary cake into a beautiful work of art. Cracks disappear beneath it; crumbs don't show through like they often do with frosting. Fondant also keeps a cake fresher longer. Amateur bakers can now produce a professional-looking cake.

Whatever kind of cake you choose, it should have an honored place at the reception with its own table (less apt to be jostled than at the head table!) and decorations. Assign someone to act as hostess to slice the cake after the first slice has been enjoyed by the bride and groom.

Food and Drink Budget Worksheet

Item	Deposit	Final Payment
Hors d'oeuvres		
Entrée		
Wait staff		
Beer		
Wine		
Soda		
Bartender		
Miscellaneous		
Glassware and Tools		
Glasses		
Ice		
Bar		
Napkins		
Miscellaneous		
Wedding Cake		
Cake		
Topper		
Cake-cutting fee		
Miscellaneous		
Total		

Chapter 6
The Clothes That Make the Wedding

Here comes the bride, all dressed in white—or not! There are absolutely no rules for what you wear on your own wedding day. You can decide the color, style, and budget for your dress. It doesn't stop there, either. You'll need accessories that complement your look, but the most important thing on your arm won't be a little bauble—it's the groom, and he needs to look sharp, too! You both need to look your best without breaking your budget.

What Will You Wear?

Don't start your search with the price tag. It's a much better idea to start looking for what will be appropriate for the location you've chosen for your ceremony.

Making a Budget for Your Dress

What budget have you set for your dress? Remember that you do not have to be bound by a smaller budget for your dress if it is one of your "priority" items for the wedding. Perhaps you want to spend more to get what you want and cut down on expenses elsewhere. This is perfectly understandable. It's an important day for you and you want to look gorgeous. After all, you'll be looking at those wedding pictures for a long, long time.

 Essential

Remember to leave money in your budget for alterations. Chances are, your dress will not fit you perfectly in some way and you'll have to have it nipped and tucked. If you have a train, you may also want to have the option to bustle it after the ceremony.

Picture Your Dress

Keep your ceremony and reception locations in mind. A big, formal dress with a sweeping train won't work if you have to walk down a grassy path outdoors for your ceremony—well, not unless you don't mind grass stains or are willing to spend the dollars to rent a runner! A dress with long sleeves for a summertime outdoor wedding won't work either. Grooms are nervous enough. They don't need to see you fainting right in front of them!

Do you want a long gown or a short one? Simple or elaborate? You can find a gown for any kind of budget, depending on your willingness to compromise. Want an elaborate gown for a little money? Consider buying a previously worn gown or a designer sample. Do you favor a simple design yet love the beadwork on a more expensive gown? Consider buying the beads from a fabric store and sewing them on yourself to save money.

Start your gown search by looking through bridal magazines and Web sites. Clip pictures of the dresses and styles you like. Also, look through any photos you can find of weddings that have taken place in the location you've chosen.

Style Guides

Countless bridal Web sites will help you decide on the dress style you prefer, so you'll know what you want when you're ready to go shopping. Doing your homework first is useful if you aren't well-versed in bridal-couture jargon.

Knowing the types of necklines and other features and whether they look good on you will also save you time and money in the bridal stores. When you speak the same language, you and the bridal consultant can work together to find what you want. You also won't be as likely to let yourself get talked into something that isn't you or that's out of your price range.

Know your silhouettes before you shop:

- **A-line gowns** are shaped like the letter A, with fitted bodices and flared skirts.
- **Ballroom gowns** are characteristic wedding gowns, with full, billowy skirts.
- **Empire-waist gowns** have a waist that starts under the bust and a slim skirt.
- **Mermaid gowns** are fitted dresses with a flare on the bottom of the skirt.
- **Sheath gowns** are formfitting dresses.

Looking for Bargains

Consignment shops are good places to find bargains. Sometimes brides buy a gown and then change their wedding date, and the gown is no longer appropriate for the new season. There you have it—a never-worn gown at reduced price!

Ask at your bridal shop whether they carry sample gowns at reduced prices. You might be lucky enough to get the gown you want at a discount. There may also be slightly damaged dresses that can be quickly and easily repaired.

Going Vintage

Although vintage shop gowns can be pricey, you can still find bargains. Especially consider this option if you are getting married in a historical setting, such as in an old local mansion. A vintage dress will complement the ambiance of the ceremony site and make you feel elegant. Gowns from the 1920s and 1930s have inspired the slinky styles fashionable today and often don't cost much. Finish the look with vintage accessories like a long string of pearls or glass beads, a beaded purse, or a period hat.

Vintage clothing is a marvelous touch for weddings of all budgets, depending on the quality and age of the garments. One caution, though—larger sizes are harder to find in vintage clothing. There may also be special cleaning or alterations that will drive up the cost.

Check the Classifieds

It's possible to find a lovely dress and stay within budget through newspaper classified ads or on online auction sites like eBay. One bride found a beautiful gown by visiting local dry cleaners, where brides have been known sometimes to abandon their dresses.

Look in Your Mother's Closet

For a priceless (in both senses of the word) opportunity, look in your mother's closet. For sentimental reasons many brides wear the gowns their mothers, grandmothers, or other female relatives wore.

If a family gown is still in good shape, you can have it professionally cleaned and altered. Occasionally, the more delicate headpieces don't survive storage, but this can be easily replicated by either you or a seamstress with the aid of wedding photos.

Question?

I love my mother's dress, but there's no way it would fit me. What can I do?
Duplicate it by finding a pattern, material, and a seamstress to stitch up a copy for you. It's a wonderful way to carry on a tradition and no one will know it's not the same gown unless you tell them!

Even Better: Free!

Do you have a friend or relative who will loan you a dress? Nothing's better than free—well, free except for what you pay to have it cleaned before you return it!

Consider sharing a gown. Two sisters shared a gown for their weddings that took place a few months apart. They loved the idea because they'd always been very close emotionally and this made for a special bond. Because of the cost savings, they were able to spend a little more for better quality. Fortunately the two were close enough in size that the second sister needed to do only minor alterations.

Something Borrowed

Renting a dress is also an option. Think of it as leasing your dream dress and not paying all that money for one use. One bride who was having a luxurious wedding decided to save money by renting her dress. "No one knew," she said afterward. "Since the rest of the wedding was so nice, it wasn't as if anyone suspected. We were able to spend the money on having a nicer reception." Check the Yellow Pages of your phone book or ask around to locate a rental source.

How to Shop—and When

Whether you use eBay or a lesser-known auction site, it's important to be a smart consumer. Be honest with yourself about sizes and preferences. Don't buy a dress that will need lots of alterations because that will eat away at whatever you've saved by purchasing your dress at auction.

 Fact

> Don't be shocked if your bridal gown size is in the double digits even if you normally wear a U.S. dress size 6 or 8. Formal dresses are often sized differently than conventional sizes. If you're worried that a dress will be too big, check your measurements against a sizing chart with your designer.

The sooner you start looking for your dress, the better. If you wait until the last minute, you're going to feel desperate and spend too much. You're also taking a chance on not finding what you want at all. Your wedding day is not the time to feel like you could be wearing something better. Start looking for a dress six to nine months before the wedding. This ensures that you have enough time to find a dress you love and have it altered in time for the wedding.

 Fact

eBay is full of wedding-gown styles at bargain prices offered by individuals as well as bridal stores. You can find tiaras under $15, gowns for $25, even a $4,000 Vera Wang worn just once for $1,500. The groom and the rest of the wedding party can find good deals there, too.

Outlets Are In

Bridal outlets are springing up in more and more cities these days. Even if you don't choose a dress bargain advertised for $99, you will find a large selection of dresses. Be careful of pressure to buy, both in the huge warehouses and in smaller specialty shops where overhead is high. If you have a year to plan your wedding, it's possible to shop at the end of a season for the new season the following year.

Be Creative

Most importantly, be creative. Keep your mind open to different solutions. Check out department stores, especially the formalwear sections, and catalogs. That simple, floor-length cocktail sheath could be a perfect wedding dress; all you need to do is add a few decorative touches.

Visit the prom dress or debutante section of formalwear stores. Many of these dresses look just like wedding dresses and cost far less.

Make It Yourself

Sewing a wedding gown might give the sewing-challenged the jitters. But take a deep breath and keep reading. Some wedding dresses are very simple, and they are indeed doable even if you aren't a seamstress. Do you have a sewing machine? That's essential. Good at reading directions? That's important, too. Willing to try? Even better.

Alert

Color is a hot trend in wedding dresses. Find a pale, pale pink or blue dress in the prom section. Add a colorful sash to a white dress from a formalwear store. Put some sparkle on a simple inexpensive dress with a fabulous pin or necklace.

If you're truly nervous, you can try buying a thin cotton material called muslin and sew together a sample of what the gown would look like. Dressmakers in years past often did this to make a custom garment. Do this to see if your achievement will look and fit the way you hope it will before you venture into buying more expensive material or spend more time trying and not being happy with your result.

Pique Your Interest

A young bride at a recent wedding made her gown of white cotton piqué trimmed with a band of lace at the neckline, sleeves, and hem. She padded a headband, wrapped it in material and sewed on a piece of lace, then attached a gathered length of tulle for a floor-length veil. It was gorgeous—so simple to sew, according to the bride, yet to us admiring onlookers it was elegant in its simplicity. She put her own wedding ensemble together for around $100.

If you find a simple sheath but want something fuller, add a billowing tulle skirt. Tulle is an ethereal, almost magical fabric, and it's easy to gather and sew. Take your waist measurement and buy several times that; you can decide how gathered you want the skirt to be. To make a matching veil, gather a shorter length and attach it to a padded headband, which you can then decorate with the same pearls, crystals, or lace as on your dress bodice.

Start Right

Start by taking your measurements to make sure to buy the right sized pattern. Some patterns cover a range of sizes (such as 10/12/14) so you can cut the top bigger or smaller than the bottom or, if you lose weight as you plan your wedding, you're not locked into a larger size. That way if you haven't cut your material and sewed it yet, later you can cut a smaller size and not have to buy another pattern.

Trimming Hides a Multitude of Sins

Don't stress if your seam isn't perfectly straight, for instance. Chances are, if you sew on a little lace appliqué here or there or add some beads or pearls, the dress will look wonderful. People are so impressed with anyone who sews that you'll be pleasantly surprised to find you'll get credit for a better job than you think you've done. You should feel proud of yourself. Making your own wedding gown is one of the most personal touches you can contribute to your day.

 Essential

Stop in a fabric store and take a look at the pattern books. You'll be pleasantly surprised to find manufacturers now making patterns for women who don't have a lot of time or who didn't learn a lot of sewing skills in a high school home-economics class.

Take a look at all the wonderful fabrics and matching trims in the fabric store, and borrow some ideas from your favorite bridal designer. If you have someone in the family who sews, invite her help. It will be a wonderful experience to sew your wedding dress together, and you'll also have someone to help you pin up the hem in the right place.

There are a number of books to guide you in sewing your own dress. *Bridal Gowns: How to Make the Wedding Dress of Your Dreams* by Susan Andriks is a good one to guide you.

About.com's *Sewing 101* lists handy resources for the beginning sewer. The Home Sewing Association's Web site, *www.sewing.org*, has a helpful section on bridal sewing.

If you decide to try making your own dress, take it one step at a time and don't invest too much money until you feel comfortable with the project. Ultimately, you need to be honest with yourself and decide whether you have the time and patience for this large undertaking. Even if all you do is make your headpiece and veil, you'll have fun being creative and will feel like you're doing something special for your wedding.

Alert

It's important to pair the right pattern with the right material. Check on the back of the pattern for suggested materials. Brocade is too stiff and formal for a relaxed style of dress, while a thin silk isn't suitable for a design that needs body.

Custom-Made Gowns

If you don't feel comfortable sewing an entire wedding gown by yourself, enlist the help of a professional seamstress to make a dress to your specifications. A custom-made gown sounds expensive, but it is often less expensive than brand-new dresses from bridal salons, and you will get exactly what you want.

Fact

> Your seamstress can work with you to design a dress that is uniquely you, but it helps both of you if you have an idea of what you want even before your first meeting. Bring pictures of wedding gowns you admire and be specific about what you want.

Find a seamstress through your network of friends and associates. Meet with her to discuss your vision. It's important that you feel a connection and are able to communicate with your seamstress so as to avoid any misunderstanding later on. If you don't feel the seamstress shares your vision for your dress, look elsewhere. Finally, ask for and check references.

Then Again, Maybe You'll Splurge

One friend was determined to help her daughter find a wedding dress that fit their budget. They had saved on everything else and were feeling pretty good about their winning streak!

As she recounts, "My daughter tried on the first one, and as she came out of the dressing room, I saw a young man with a young woman looking at dresses. I don't know if she was his fiancée or friend, but anyway, he shook her arm to get her attention and said, 'Oh, wow, look at her!' Now, the other young woman wasn't real happy at that remark at first, but she looked at my daughter and you could see she thought it made Sarah a beautiful bride.

"The dress was twice the budget we wanted to spend. I could tell Sarah thought this was 'The Dress,' you know, the one that they say you'll just know is It. She said that she could be happy with the dress that was more in our budget, but I just couldn't let her. We decided we'd find some way to save in other places." And they did.

 Essential

Many bridal salons request that you call ahead to make an appointment to try dresses on. This allows them to plan for your visit and give you individualized attention.

Find Other Places to Save

"There was a headpiece to match the dress, and the price was outrageous," added Sarah. "It just bothered me to see what they wanted for a simple cloth scrunchy-looking thing that wrapped around my topknot. I mean, it was really just a ponytail holder! I made a satin one to match my gown and attached a fingertip-length veil to it, and no one was the wiser. I spent next to nothing for the small amount of satin and the tulle for the veil."

Sample Sales

Sample sales are a smart way to buy a designer gown at a discount price. Bridal salons sell sample gowns once the manufacturer discontinues them, usually a seasonal occurrence. Bridal salons take great care to keep their samples in good condition, but usually they will have been tried on by a number of customers. Slight imperfections are unavoidable, but you can replace a zipper, have the sample dress professionally cleaned, and still come out ahead.

 Fact

If you are even reasonably adept with a needle or a glue gun, you can put together a headpiece that won't cost as much as the ready-made ones. Visit the bridal section at your local fabric or craft store.

Three Choices

You may have a vision of the dress you want, but remember that the time, place, and formality of a particular wedding determines what kind of gown is appropriate. The suitability of the gown for the setting of your ceremony is as important to its overall effect as how it actually looks on you.

A Dress for a Country Club Wedding

"I didn't want something as fussy and formal as if I'd been getting married in a church," Lynn said. "And, of course, it had to be elegant and easy to dance in." She chose a short, ivory candlelight dress and added a chiffon stole that will flutter in the breeze off the water as she and John walk along the wooden deck of the marina country club.

 Fact

> Helping the bride find a dress is usually the maid of honor's task, but you will probably find no shortage of friends and family members to go dress shopping with you. Take only one or two people with you at a time. It's easy to get overwhelmed by all the opinions if you go in a large group.

A Dress for a Traditional Church Wedding

Opting for the traditional, Kylie selected a dress with a cathedral-length train but found it in an unorthodox source—a wedding-finery rental store. "I never thought I'd do this," she confided. "But when I realized I could get something so special for a fraction of the cost, I did it." The rental cost Kylie just $275, instead of the $1,200 she had budgeted.

Super Savings on a Small Wedding

Susan has had a hectic last semester at college and couldn't spare a lot of time to look around for her dress. "I studied the pictures of summer weddings held outdoors and realized that those dresses wouldn't work in my setting—or my budget! So I started looking for a simpler kind of dress, with a tea-length hem that wouldn't brush the grass—something that would carry out my fresh, outdoor theme. There was a dress online that looked perfect for a summer wedding. I bid on it and got it for $75!"

But something was missing. "I'd been looking at the bride magazines and saw that hats were becoming popular again," Susan said. "So I splurged on a beautiful wide-brimmed hat and trimmed it with some silk daisies to match the real ones I'd be carrying in my bouquet. I sewed a few on the hem of the dress, and I had a beautiful outfit."

Remember that alterations can add quite a bit to the price of your purchased gown, especially if you lose weight and require multiple fittings and alterations. Be sure to get a written estimate of the cost and try not to go through drastic size changes. After all, that's not good for your health, and you have enough stress in your life now, anyway!

 Alert

This point can't be stressed enough: Wherever you shop, remember to be a wise consumer and use that credit card. It will give you more leverage if the order isn't what you expected.

Saving on Wedding Gown Accessories

Once you have picked your gown, you also need to consider matching shoes and jewelry as well as other accessories—for example, a hat, a shawl, or a veil.

Shoes for Walking Down the Aisle

For your special day, you'll want new shoes, of course. But don't think you have to go for those pricey white satin ones you find in the bridal stores. Begin your search at discount stores, and look in the regular shoe section of any footwear or department store for shoes that complement your gown. If you like, dress them up with clip-on shoe jewelry available at these stores. Whatever type of shoes you choose, try to buy some that you can wear after the wedding.

 Fact

Make sure you pick out a pair of shoes you find comfortable, since you're going to be on your feet a lot on your wedding day. The same is true for your attendants: Don't force your bridesmaids to hobble down the aisle in shoes they might not feel at ease in.

Save the money you might be tempted to spend on overly decorated shoes that you'll wear just once—unless they're a high-priority item for you. Also remember that you don't have to get expensive dyeable shoes that you probably won't wear again. Check out the shoes you want to wear for comfort. There are many adorable styles that have low or flat heels, which are especially necessary for outdoor weddings!

Jewels for a Price

If you've been given a necklace by your fiancé or parents, you already have special jewelry to wear for the wedding. If you don't have something that seems ideal, a simple strand of pearls or a chain with a drop pearl is an elegant and risk-free option. You'll find items like these for any budget in the costume jewelry sections of department stores and other shops. If you usually prefer jewelry in a different style, don't spend the money for genuine pearls you may not wear very often.

 Essential

Take a look at museum gift-shop catalogs that feature reproductions of exquisite, work-of-art jewelry at reasonable prices. You can make an inexpensive selection that will give you a megabucks look.

Lingerie

No one's going to see them but the groom, but you still need to think about your undergarments. Decide whether you need any special hosiery for your dress and whether you'll don a garter. You can try to go with items you already have in your closet, but if the bras and undergarments you own aren't suitable, you might have to invest in new ones. Make sure whatever you select is comfortable and offers adequate support since you'll be wearing it the entire day.

Hairstyles and Makeup

Everyone has seen the bride who decides to use her wedding to try out a new look that just isn't her—whether it's a new hairstyle or just too much makeup. Ask your stylist to arrange a good time to get your haircut, body perm, or hair color so that it looks its best for your wedding. You don't want any unpleasant surprises on your wedding day! If your hair wilts or turns frizzy on a damp day, discuss a backup plan for a different style.

Do a test run with your stylist before the wedding, taking your veil, flowers, or whatever headpiece you're using with you. It's also a good idea to bring a photo of your wedding dress so you can both agree on a look that suits you best.

 Alert

The groom should also be careful not to let his barber get carried away with the scissors and give him a cut that's too short just before the wedding. One bride confided that she never knew her new husband had such big ears—they were revealed when he got his new haircut a few days before the wedding!

Think about consulting with a makeup expert at a counter in an upscale department store for advice on what colors and type of makeup to wear for different times of the day or season. You'll get some free advice on what looks good. Just be careful not to go overboard and buy expensive makeup you won't use again.

Now for the Groom

Who's looked at as much as the bride on the wedding day? Why, the groom, of course! And while he may be the handsomest man on the planet, some of the styles in the men's formalwear shop just don't cut it, do they? Some men look great in casual wear but look uncomfortable in a cutaway, and other men love a chance to look dashing in formalwear.

All tuxes are not made alike. There are vastly different styles that flatter different body types. If the groom doesn't want you to go with him, perhaps his best man and his attendants can do so. As one men's formalwear Web site warns, neither you nor your fiancé wants him to walk out of the store with a polyester bell-bottom set from the 1970s.

 Fact

Look out for discounts for the groom. The groom's tuxedo may come free if the groomsmen rent their tuxes from the same rental place. The groom can also help trim costs from the budget by forgoing extras like new shoes. Be aware that there could be surcharges if the groom or his groomsmen order their tuxes less than four weeks before the wedding.

Check Bridal Magazines for Him, Too

Glance through bridal magazines to get a sense of what type of men's formalwear is appropriate for the type of wedding you're having, and then consult with your local tuxedo-rental store. The biggest designers for men are Ralph Lauren, Tommy Hilfiger, Perry Ellis, and FUBU. Tuxes made by these designers are also available for sale.

The rules dictating what type of tux should be worn at which time of day are no longer operative. Just like women, men are refusing to be ruled by fashion tyrants. Wearing a tux is not even necessary. A simple, good-quality suit in black or dark gray (even brown for summer) is appropriate for many weddings. If you're having a Western wedding, for example, then you might want to go with a Texas formal style: tuxedo jackets with new jeans and a Stetson hat.

 Essential

A visit to eBay might encourage your fiancé to buy a tux rather than rent one. Men's sizes tend to be more consistent than women's, so sizing shouldn't be much of a problem. If attending more formal events is in your future together, it makes more financial sense to buy a tux rather than rent one.

Virtual Shopping

Sit down with your fiancé and take a look at some of the Web sites that feature tuxedo-rental stores. Good ones to check out are *www.afterhours.com* and *www.marrying man.com*. The latter flashes you a reminder of how many days left until "the Big Day" and encourages grooms to "Do It Now"—order the tux, that is!). You can look through the sites together and see what styles and colors would be appropriate for your wedding.

Dressing the Bride Budget Worksheet

Use this handy worksheet to document expenses for your wedding. Keeping track of everything you spend will ensure that you stay within your budget. You might want to make a copy of the worksheet and tuck it into your purse or daily calendar so you remember to make entries as soon as you make the purchases. You might need to customize this worksheet a bit, depending on your particular wedding plans.

Clothing for the bride

Dress:	$_____
Headpiece:	$_____
Shoes:	$_____
Undergarments and pantyhose:	$_____
Hairdresser and makeup:	$_____
Miscellaneous:	$_____

Clothing for the groom

Tuxedo rental or purchase:	$_____
Shoes:	$_____

Underwear and socks: $_____

Miscellaneous

_____: $_____
_____: $_____
_____: $_____
_____: $_____

Total: **$_____**

Chapter 7
Here Comes the Wedding Party

Here they come—those dear friends and family members who make up your wedding party. Whether you have just a few people or a large number of attendants, each one is important to you and plays a special part in your day. This is perhaps the only day for which you have the pleasure of picking out clothes for adults, and there are numerous factors that go along with this responsibility.

Budgeting for the Wedding Party

Before you ask those attendants to be part of your day, it's important to take a look at your budget. While the bride and groom are not responsible for paying for the attire of their wedding party, you still have to consider your finances. At the very least, each attendant means a bouquet or boutonniere, a meal at the rehearsal dinner and at the reception, transportation expenses to the reception, and a gift for participating.

 Fact

Traditionally, there is a ratio between the number of attendants and the total number of guests who are invited to the wedding: one bridesmaid and one groomsman for every thirty to fifty guests. When it comes down to it, it's up to you. You can have twenty attendants or none at all.

Then, too, it's important for the bride and groom to think about how expenses may add up for their attendants. Each attendant must pay for the dress or the rental tux, special shoes, and accessories. There may be transportation costs and possibly even hotel stays. Attendants may have to miss work to attend the events or at the very least, time to attend rehearsals and so on. Therefore, it's important for the bride and groom to carefully look at budgets—both theirs and those of their prospective attendants.

Dressing the Bridesmaids

Bridesmaids are the bride's attendants, the prelude to her walk down the aisle, a part of her inner circle on her special day. They deserve to look and feel their best. Unfortunately, they often hate what they have to wear. We've all seen some of these dresses and wondered what the bride was thinking.

 Essential

The groomsmen usually rent their wedding-day attire, and there's no reason the bridesmaids shouldn't do the same. Renting bridesmaid dresses saves your attendants valuable cash. Find a local shop that specializes in renting special occasion wear.

Even if every bridesmaid wears the same dress size, they will each have different physical shapes and skin tones. So choosing the right dresses for the bridesmaids can be a daunting task. Finding identical dresses that look right on different persons takes attention on top of everything else you have to decide. Often the bride chooses a color scheme for her wedding that becomes the color range for the bridesmaids' gowns.

First, Pick the Color

Seasons dictate certain colors. For spring, colors like pastel pinks, blues, greens, and yellows are popular, while summer colors are stronger and more vibrant. Fall colors deepen into more earthy tones like golds, russets, and browns. Winter colors include reds and greens, silver and gold, purple, and darker blues. And black? Black is a year-round favorite. It can be used even in summer for a dramatic, sophisticated bridal-attendant dress. White is another possibility, but many brides shun it for their attendants since they will wear it as the traditional center of attention. No matter what the season, using your favorite color is always a rewarding choice.

Look at the Style

One of the reasons bridesmaids' gowns have been so hated is that they look like bridesmaids' gowns. The idea these days is to make the dress something that can be worn again. Try not to choose something that's fussy, with big puffy sleeves or skirt or something that obviously labels it as a dress that was worn for a wedding.

The style of the bride's gown often determines that of her attendants. If you're wearing a sleek, floor-length sheath, try to pick bridesmaids' gowns that mirror your look. Wearing an A-line gown with an empire waist? That can be the gown style you seek for your maid of honor and bridesmaids.

Consider your bridesmaids' body types, and choose a style that suits all of them. Remember, you aren't shopping for yourself. If you're small-chested and can pull off a strapless dress with minimal bra support, keep in mind that your future sister-in-law and her 36Ds may not thank you for picking that style.

Bargain Bridesmaid Dresses

New brides are the best source of advice for planning your wedding. If you know anyone who's recently gotten married or is a few months ahead of you in planning a wedding, ask her where she bought her bridesmaid dresses. You'll get recommendations and possibilities you might not have thought of.

 Essential

A-line gowns basically look like the letter *A*: fitted bodice, natural waist, and flared skirt. They are flattering for almost every body type. Empire waists begin directly under a fitted bodice. Be aware that they can make heavier women look pregnant, although the style works for most bridesmaids.

Bridal Salons

You can find some great deals at the bridal salon where you bought your wedding gown. Sometimes, bridesmaid dress prices will be adjusted if your wedding gown is pricey or if you order a certain number of bridesmaid gowns. Ask about this when you go to buy your gown. Remember that if you're planning your wedding far in advance, your attendants can take advantage of end-of-season sales. Stick with a classic style and it won't be outdated when your wedding takes place.

Make Your Own

Even better, hire someone to make your bridesmaid dresses. You may be able to find someone to sew dresses more cheaply than you could buy them. Find a seamstress experienced in sewing bridesmaid dresses by looking in the Yellow Pages under "Alterations," then ask to see some of her work. Be sure to set a realistic deadline for completing and fitting the dresses before the wedding.

Nontraditional Bridesmaid Dresses

A bridesmaid dress doesn't have to have "bridesmaid" written on the tag or be located in the bridesmaid section of your wedding salon. Try looking in the prom section of department stores. Prom dresses haven't looked sweet and innocent in many years. Today's prom dresses are smart and stylish and are well-suited to women over high school age.

 Essential

Go bridesmaid-dress shopping with no more than one or two of your attendants at a time. The fewer people accompanying you, the easier it will be to reach a decision. Try to go with the bridesmaids most representative of your attendant group to get a sense of how different dresses will look on different people.

Evening wear can double as bridesmaid wear. You'll find dresses of every description that can be wonderful for a wedding. Look for simple, classic designs, and let the saleswoman know you want the dresses for your bridesmaids. She'll be able to guide you to appropriate styles—nothing too revealing or too sexy. Some evening gowns come with matching jackets or wraps, which is a nice bonus, especially if the outfit is to be worn in the cooler months.

Question?

The bridesmaid gowns we bought look too simple. How can we fix them?

Add gorgeous satin sashes—maybe even tie one on your wedding gown—or try some metallic belts. Jeweled appliqués are simple to sew on for drama and are budget friendly, too. Add brooches or pins for just a touch of sparkle to punch up a dull dress.

For best selection, ask when the store gets its seasonal shipments. Many retail stores offer a discount when you open a store credit card, and this purchase is a good chance to take advantage of that opportunity.

Saving Time

Let your bridesmaids know what color and/or style you have decided on and let each woman choose her own dress. You'll spend less time agonizing over finding a dress to suit everyone, and you won't have to deal with bridesmaids whining to you about how alarmingly fat they'll look in the dress you chose. Each bridesmaid will be able to pick the dress that suits her best, and everyone will be happy.

 Fact

When you look for gowns for your attendants, check out two-piece gowns. You can mix and match different bodice types with different skirts. You'll get variety, a better fit, and savings on alterations since your attendants can pick a different size for the tops and skirts.

Kylie chose a teal organdy fabric for her bridesmaids and an aquamarine shade of the same fabric for her matron of honor. Then each attendant picked out a dress style that best suited her. The maid of honor, a tall, slim blonde, found a halter-neck A-line gown. The pregnant matron of honor loved the two-piece gown she found in the maternity section of a catalog; the portrait collar brought attention to her face, while the top was cut to flow smoothly over her tummy. She found it so flattering that she planned to have the floor-length skirt cut to knee-length to wear to another function later that season. The other two bridesmaids happened to be twins, and they chose empire-waist gowns with spaghetti straps to accentuate their tans.

Affordable Accessories

Once you've decided on the bridesmaid dresses, it's time to find accessories that don't break the budget. It's best not to overdo the accessories. Find some stylish but comfortable shoes, a wrap, and some light jewelry for a classic look.

Shoes

Shoes are a challenge. For a uniform look, you can pick out one pair of shoes and ask each bridesmaid to buy a pair in her size. This means more work for you, unfortunately, and some bridesmaids might grumble about style, comfort, and price.

For a semi-uniform look, you can ask your bridesmaids to wear a certain color and allow them to pick their own shoes. Try to pick a color your bridesmaids will wear again. Metallic shades are popular, and they are appropriate for many bridesmaid dresses.

That's a Wrap!

Shawls, stoles, and wraps can be a lovely accessory for a wedding—and a necessity if you get married on a chilly day. If you're having the attendants' gowns made, buy extra fabric and have matching wraps sewn. The cost will be low, but the look will be rich. Retail stores tend to place wraps on sale after holidays and proms. Your attendants will thank you, especially if their gowns are strapless or have spaghetti straps. Even the young and toned don't always like their shoulders and arms.

The Guys' Turn

Once the groom's tux is picked out, a similar look is in order for the men in his party. A popular look for the men is to pick up the color of the bridesmaids' gowns in their tie or cummerbund. Tread carefully if you've chosen pink; some of the men may object. But in general, the men attending the groom seem to be the easiest to please.

 Essential

Cuff links are a popular gift for groomsmen. You can give the groomsmen their gifts at the rehearsal dinner so they can show off their new accessories on your wedding day.

Follow the Groom

In general, the tuxes for the groomsmen should be similar in style to the groom's tux. If the groom is going very formal, then it follows that the groomsmen need to be styled similarly. Likewise, if the wedding is more informal, the attire worn should be informal like the groom's.

Following the style set by the groom, the groomsmen need shirts and cummerbunds or vests that match those of the groom. Bow ties or regular ties should also match. Tuxedo-rental shops can take care of the whole package for the groomsmen: tuxedo, cummerbunds or vests, and shoes.

Groomsmen have more leeway when it comes to timing. They don't absolutely need to place their orders until two or three months before the wedding, but it helps to place your order early. No one wants to find himself competing for a tux with the local high school prom-goers.

Fact

Generally, all men in the wedding party order their formal-wear from the same store to make certain that their look is consistent. Some stores also offer a discount package, such as a special rate for the groom's tux rental.

Ditch the Tuxes

Tuxes aren't strictly necessary. If you are having an informal wedding, opt for blazers instead of tuxes. You can rent suits or ask each groomsman to wear one he already owns. Tie the look together with matching ties or pocket squares. For extremely informal weddings, groomsmen can even forget the blazer. Ask them to wear khakis, and buy matching printed shirts to distinguish them as groomsmen.

Me! Me!—Dressing the Child Attendants

Is there anything more adorable than the smallest members of the wedding party? We're talking precious little girls all dressed up, their hair styled in "princess" hairdos, walking down the aisle scattering rose petals. Then there are those handsome little boys in miniature tuxes carrying the wedding rings tied to a ring pillow.

While you can never be quite sure about how they'll behave that day—they are, after all, children—you can depend on having them be a very special part of your day. Since parents have enough expenses, they'll appreciate your help in keeping down the costs of the clothing.

Not Just Playing Dress Up

You can find flower-girl and junior-bridesmaid dresses in a bridal store, of course, but also in the regular children's section of a department store, especially at holiday time. A dress that's displayed for a Christmas party can be wonderful for a wedding, too. Ask the parent to buy the dress in the size she anticipates the child will be when the wedding takes place. Prices for holiday dresses, especially through after-holiday sales, can be a significant savings. Pageant stores can also be a source of dresses for a flower girl.

 Essential

You can buy patterns for flower-girl dresses at any fabric store. Hire a seamstress to make a dress or find a talented friend or family member to do it for free. These dresses are often less complicated than bridesmaid dresses, so people who don't feel comfortable sewing five bridesmaid dresses may be more willing to make a flower-girl dress.

Looks for children tend to stay in style for a long time. You would be safe, for instance, in using a dress worn in a wedding a few years earlier, perhaps by a sibling or a cousin. Some dresses can even be dyed a different color for a fresh look. Try adding a new sash in a color to match the bridal attendants or sew some silk flowers or sparkly trim on an old dress to add charm.

Ring bearers, like the groomsmen, are easier to shop for. You can buy or rent a little tuxedo at a bridal salon. For a more casual look, you can buy a regular suit at a department store or let the ring bearer wear a suit he already owns. Buy him a tie to match the groomsmen so that he'll fit right in.

Go Online for Bargains

eBay and other online auctions are an invaluable source of formalwear for little girls and boys. The clothing has usually been worn just one time. Some bridal-wear and formalwear stores also sell new items online. Either way, the seller must state whether the clothing is new or used. Remember that you can always have clothing professionally dry-cleaned if you buy it used.

Baskets and Pillows

Bridal salons strategically lay out flower-girl baskets and ring-bearer pillows for brides to notice when they shop for themselves. However, you can easily save money by buying or renting these items yourself.

You'll find baskets in all sizes at any crafts store, which you can spray-paint whatever color you like and then attach ribbons to the handles to make them fancier. For a variation of the traditional flower-girl image, you can forgo the basket and let your flower girl carry a minibouquet or pomander.

Making your own pillow for your ring bearer ensures that you save money and get the design you like the best. You can pick the fabric and color you prefer and accent it with ribbons or appliqués. There's no rule that says the ring bearer needs a pillow, either. You can have him carry the rings in a jewelry box you inherited from your great-grandmother or another piece that has a special significance for you or your fiancé.

Dressing the Bridal Party Budget Worksheet

Use this handy worksheet to document expenses for your wedding. Keeping track of everything you spend will ensure that you stay within your budget. You might want to make a copy of the worksheet and tuck it into your purse or daily calendar so you remember to make entries as soon as you make the purchases. You might need to customize this worksheet a bit, depending on your particular wedding plans.

Clothing for the maid/matron of honor

Dress:	$_____
Headpiece:	$_____
Shoes:	$_____
Undergarments and pantyhose:	$_____
Hairdresser and makeup:	$_____

Clothing for bridesmaid #1

Dress:	$_____
Headpiece:	$_____
Shoes:	$_____
Undergarments and pantyhose:	$_____
Hairdresser and makeup:	$_____

Clothing for bridesmaid # 2

Dress:	$_____
Headpiece:	$_____
Shoes:	$_____
Undergarments and pantyhose:	$_____
Hairdresser and makeup:	$_____

Clothing for the best man

Tux rental or purchase:	$_____
Shoes:	$_____
Underwear and socks:	$_____

Clothing for groom's attendants

Tux rental or purchase:	$_____
Shoes:	$_____
Underwear and socks:	$_____

Miscellaneous

_____:	$_____
_____:	$_____

_____: $_____
_____: $_____

Total: $_____

Chapter 8
Words for Inviting; Flowers to Delight In

You're getting ready to spread the good news. The time has come to think about the invitations and the message you want to send your honored guests. At the same time, reflect on the flowers you want for your bouquet and decorations. Enjoy the process of finding the perfect flowers for the perfect price.

Sending Out the Announcements

You don't have to be content with the one or two books of samples offered by a bored teenaged clerk at the local stationery store. It's easy to find save-the-dates and invitations with a personal touch. Now that you've decided on a time, date, and location for your wedding, finally seeing the details in print can give you an exciting feeling that it's really going to happen.

Save that Date!

Formerly reserved exclusively for guests who needed to travel long distances or for weddings scheduled on holiday weekends, save-the-dates are an increasingly popular way of getting the word out about your wedding, no matter when it is or who is invited.

 Essential

Save-the-date cards don't necessarily have to be actual cards. Creative couples order save-the-date magnets so their guests can remember the upcoming event every time they get milk out of the refrigerator. They can cost as little as twenty cents per magnet.

Save-the-dates are usually sent six months before the wedding. A piece of paper mailed with your names, your wedding date, and your wedding location might seem like a frivolous waste of money, but it can help your guests start planning all of their travel arrangements. You can also use this as an opportunity to pass along information about local hotels, discount rates, and wedding attire.

 Alert

When you add up save-the-date notices, invitations, and response cards, postage will be a significant expense. Be sure it's included in your budget. If you don't figure it in, you will think you're on target with your budget, but when you sit down to add everything up—ouch!

One inexpensive option is to send digital save-the-dates to your guests' e-mail addresses. Wedding Web sites such as The Knot (*www.theknot.com*) offer free electronic save-the-dates. If you prefer physical save-the-date cards, consider designing them yourself and printing them on your home computer. The only expenses will be paper, ink, and postage. Some stationery retailers offer discounts for couples who buy both their save-the-dates and invitations at the same place.

You're Invited!

Traditional invitations include outer and inner envelopes, the invitation itself, a reception card, a response card, and maps or directions to the ceremony and reception sites. Order them four months before the wedding and send them out six to eight weeks before the big day.

Let your wedding style and budget guide you as you pick out your wedding invitations. Your invitations let your guests catch a glimpse of your wedding's style and degree of formality. However, remember that options that make your invitations fancier, such as special trims like lace or appliques or specialty papers, add to the expense and may require additional postage.

Be mindful of your budget when ordering the number of invitations, too. It's best to order an additional two dozen invitations in case you suddenly remember guests you should have invited. You may also want to give an extra invitation to your parents or members of your wedding party to include in photo or memory books. A nice touch after the wedding is to give a small album to the parents of the bride and groom. Paste the invitation on the cover, hot-glue decorations around it, and fill the inside with photos of the wedding.

Question?

What can we do with extra invitations?
Use your extra invitations to create gifts for your wedding party. Cut out pictures of you with your friends in the wedding party, paste them around the invitations, frame the collages, and present them to your bridesmaids and groomsmen.

Extra invitations and envelopes are helpful if there's a mistake in addressing them or some are returned for an incorrect address and you need to resend them. No one wants to have to go back to the printer with a small order and pay for express service or express mail.

Be careful with those extra invitations. Don't fall into the trap of saying, "Oh, let's invite so-and-so," and little by little expand your guest list. Your wedding and reception should be reserved for people who are really important to you. No matter what the size of your budget, don't invite people for any other reason.

Finding Invitations

Start by finding stationery suppliers. Set aside time to sit and look through samples. You can visit local stationery suppliers or opt for virtual shopping. Web sites offer a multiplicity of invitation styles, prices, and creative touches to suit any budget. Just type "wedding invitations" into your favorite search engine and links to hundreds of sites will appear, many of which offer the same name brands carried by the best stationery stores. Prices can be anywhere from 15 to 30 percent lower than those from a local store, though be sure to consider shipping costs in dealing with an online stationery service.

If you're unsure of what you want, certain wedding Web sites and bridal-magazine sites show galleries of wedding invitations. Free catalogs and samples are available, and many companies offer to send you a proof of your invitation to make sure you're totally happy before you complete your order.

Express Yourself

You want your invitation to be different from everyone else's, but you also don't want to spend a lot of money. Stay with the least expensive cardstock and printing options, and then add your own unique features with a special or customized sealing stamp or ribbon that you can attach yourself.

 Alert

Watch out: Wedding-invitation suppliers are banking on you becoming so enthused that you end up ordering hundreds of dollars of their merchandise. The list of extras available, such as fancy ribbons and printing, foil papers, or pressed flowers, is astonishing. Before you agree to extra combinations, ask yourself whether you really need all those features.

DIY Invitations

You can make your own wedding invitations. Buy kits at office-supply or stationery stores and design them at home. All you need is a little time and a good printer—no artistic ability required. You can design your own invitations using a word processing program, then print them out and assemble them. Invitation kits come with everything you need, including response cards and envelopes. Paper Source (*www.paper-source.com*) has unique kits and ideas for do-it-yourself invitations.

Special Touches

One bride and groom who were having a medieval-style wedding printed their invitations on 8½-by-11-inch pieces of ivory paper, which they rolled and tied with ribbons: voilà, scroll invitations! They cost a little more to mail because they needed mailing tubes, but the couple felt the effect was worth the extra expense.

Another bride who was getting married in a Victorian mansion wanted more elaborate invitations without spending a lot. She chose rose-colored paper, a fancy font, and glued pressed flowers and lace medallions on the invitations.

 Fact

Make sure you factor in *all* of the paper-related expenses you'll rack up for your wedding, including ceremony programs and thank-you cards. You can buy thank-you cards in bulk from your stationer. Menus for each place setting at the reception are also a nice touch.

One couple invited their guests to a Western-style wedding with a chambray-blue invitation sporting a rope border encircling the text. Think about a theme for your wedding. Is there a way to have fun conveying it by way of your invitation? You're planning a wedding at the beach. . . . Doesn't that setting lend itself to invitations that convey a seaside mood? Try to find invitations that set the style and tone of your wedding without adding significant expense.

Our Three Couples

After looking at several stationery stores and Web sites, Susan and Nick thought about designing their own invitations but realized they didn't really have enough time to do so. However, they remembered that a friend of theirs, a recent computer graphics graduate, often did freelance work for local businesses to help pay his tuition. The friend is working with them on a simple invitation design featuring Susan's daisy-themed wedding. A local office-supply store will do the printing for a very reasonable price.

Kylie and Sean wanted invitations to suit their traditional wedding, including reception cards and special touches like wax seals closing the envelope. They opted for a local stationer to whom they were willing to pay a little extra for invitations that set the formal tone of their wedding.

 Essential

Some couples include their e-mail addresses on their invitations, allowing guests to R.S.V.P. electronically. People are so busy these days, it's often easier for them to respond by e-mail. Personalized wedding Web sites give you the option to let guests respond online, too.

From the deck of the marina country club where they're having their wedding and reception, Lynn and John took a photograph of a gorgeous sunset, which they had reproduced on their wedding invitation with a foil seal of the club on the envelope. Kylie admitted the invitations were pricey, but added, "They're so beautiful, an aunt has already framed hers and sent it to us as a gift for our home."

Budget Buds

Weddings and flowers—they just go together. Many of us remember the flowers from weddings we've attended: the fragrant white roses of the bride's bouquet, the garden wedding site that's a symphony of color and scent, the little baskets of lily of the valley at the reception tables.

 Fact

Some brides are allergic to flowers, so they opt to carry as well as decorate with silk flowers. Just remember that it can be as expensive to have a florist supply and arrange silk flowers as fresh ones.

Budget Wisely

Flowers can make a wedding. They can also break your budget if you're not careful. How much you choose to spend and what portion of the budget you allot is totally up to you. Some sources suggest that flowers are the second biggest expense after reception food and drink, but they don't have to be. If flowers aren't a high priority for you, set a smaller budget for them and spend your money where you want to.

Map out exactly where you want flowers. If the site of either the ceremony or reception is in an already lavishly decorated space, you may need few if any floral arrangements. If you do need them for both locales, figure out whether the flowers from the ceremony can be taken to the reception site as well. You also need to decide what to do about bouquets, boutonnieres, and corsages. If you decide to forgo the bouquets, you and your bridesmaids can walk down the aisle with fans or parasols. Consider making the boutonnieres for the groom, groomsmen, and fathers yourself.

DIY Flowers

If you'd like to do any part of the flower arrangements yourself, find a wholesaler like Costco or visit a flower market or flea market for bargains. Look for locally grown varieties for the best savings. Rent vases from local florists or buy inexpensive ones from the dollar store. Do a test run before the wedding to make sure you feel comfortable assembling a flower arrangement.

If you want to save money on flowers but feel clueless when it comes to working with real or silk flowers, don't despair. Ready-made arrangements are available at many decorating stores; some even have designers who can make what you want from silk flowers and greenery you purchase at the store.

Check to see whether you'll be charged for such an arrangement. If there is a charge, it's usually reasonable compared to ordering from a florist. Some florists don't mind mixing silk and real flowers, but the price won't differ much; it's the labor that's usually more expensive than the blooms.

Choosing a Florist: Saving Time and Money

To find a florist you will be pleased with, get referrals from others. Ask past customers whether the flowers they ended up with were the ones they had ordered. Make sure there were no unexpected, expensive add-ons.

 Alert

Stick to your budget, and be wary of anyone who tries to convince you that you must spend a fortune to get what you want. Careful planning, a willingness to compromise, and sometimes doing the work yourself can save you a lot of money.

Interview the Florist

When you have your preliminary list, try to visit two or three florists before making a choice. Ask lots of questions about what you want, and pay attention to how you're treated. If the florist is not willing to spend a few minutes discussing what you want, you have not found the vendor for you.

Come prepared with pictures of bouquets and arrangements you like that you've clipped from magazines, and ask whether the florist can duplicate the look. If you feel patted on the head and gently encouraged to choose from a few photos of standard bouquets or a prepackaged floral-arrangement album, you're in the wrong place.

Ask to see pictures of the flowers the florist has done for past weddings, which will give you an idea of the florist's style. Even if this doesn't match your own, a good florist is still able to make your vision a reality. Tell him what you have in mind for your wedding and ask whether he has any suggestions. Ask him how he will approach your wedding and whether you will be able to see advance samples of your bouquets and arrangements. Other questions to ask a prospective florist include:

- What flower arrangement that you designed are you happiest with and why?
- How many weddings do you normally do on a single weekend? Will you have time to give our wedding the attention it deserves?
- Have you designed arrangements for weddings at our ceremony and reception sites before?
- Will you provide the vases and urns or will we need to rent them from a third party?
- Will you deliver and set up the large arrangements? How long do you need to set up?
- Will the flowers we like be in season? If not, what substitutions do you recommend?
- How expensive are the flowers we like? If they are too expensive, are there less expensive options that will look just as good?
- How soon do we need to put down a deposit?

Make sure you arrange for the flowers to be picked up or delivered. When recent bride Eva had a relative doing her flowers and the woman's check bounced, Eva couldn't get the bouquets and arrangements.

"We didn't find out until the evening before the wedding! Then it was too late to run to the florist for help. We had to scramble to find another alternative at the last minute and was it ever expensive!" Eva related.

Sealing the Deal

The final step is to make certain you get the transaction details in writing. You should have a written agreement spelling out the price of the flowers and the style of the arrangements. Also put in writing when the florist will deliver the flowers for your ceremony and reception so there is no misunderstanding or excuse for undelivered flowers. Ask whether the florist will set the arrangements in place and stay to pin on boutonnieres and corsages.

Choosing the Flowers

Many people are all thumbs with flowers and barely know the names of different plants. Such people are happy to leave flower designing and arranging to the florist, but even florists need direction to ensure you're happy with the final product. Here are some ideas you might like to consider.

Handy Flower Guides

One bride looked through several issues of bridal magazines to get an idea of the kinds of flowers and bouquet shapes available during her wedding season. She learned the difference between a cascade bouquet, an arm bouquet, a nosegay, and a pomander. Her familiarity with the terminology saved time when she went to the florist and kept her from having unrealistic expectations.

"I didn't see certain flowers in the issues, so when I met with the florist, the first question I asked was, 'Why?' She explained that they weren't readily available, so I didn't get my heart set on them and then get disappointed."

 Essential

Flower girls traditionally walk down the aisle scattering petals as they go. An alternative is to give your flower girl a basket of whole flowers she can simply carry. Some ceremony sites prefer the less-messy option.

Since she was having a traditional wedding, the florist showed her an album of bouquets and table arrangements suited to that type of wedding. She knew she had the right florist when the woman urged her to carry a smaller bouquet because of her petite size. "She explained that I was supposed to be the focal point, not the flowers I carried."

The satisfied bride also offers another tip: "We also saved having the flowers taken from the church and sent on to the reception site. That was a service that the florist suggested, something I hadn't thought of, and it helped us save the expense of ordering additional flowers for the reception site."

 Fact

Martha Stewart Weddings magazine demystifies the process of making your own simple bouquets. Check out *www.marthastewart.com/weddings* for more information on wedding flowers and other features designed to help you have a stylish and affordable wedding.

"I wanted white roses but didn't want to pay a lot," said Ingrid, a winter bride. "The cost was awful. Then I realized that I could carry one long-stemmed rose wrapped in silk ribbon. The bridesmaids did the same. Guests later told me that we looked so elegant." It's quality—not quantity—that counts!

Special Floral Effects

Weddings that have a medieval, Victorian, or Western flavor dictate their own color schemes and flowers. Ivy and wildflowers are evocative of medieval times, while rose and lace nosegays are suitable for a Victorian theme. Western brides take their inspiration from regional flowers and casual bouquet shapes.

Small Elements Have Big Appeal

Small single decorations such as votive candles in glass holders or glass flowerpots filled with blooms are inexpensive touches that add gaiety to any wedding. They can also serve double duty as party favors. For modest budgets, look in dollar stores for cute little glass flowerpots and votives in bundles of one hundred. These items are also on sale at craft stores and discount superstores. For moderate-budget weddings, look in department stores for fancier glass votive holders and candles. For truly lavish weddings, think about bowls with floating candles every few place settings on the tables.

 Essential

Add seasonal elements to your centerpieces. In addition to using seasonal flowers to keep prices down, pay tribute to the time of year by incorporating small buds in the spring or colorful leaves in the autumn.

Out of the Ordinary

Given their luxurious budget, John and Lynn wanted special flower arrangements. "We chose orchids for my bouquet, not just because I love them, but because they'll remind me that right after the wedding, we're leaving for our honeymoon in Hawaii," Lynn explained. "My florist looked at a picture of my gown and suggested orchids. But we didn't need a whole bouquet of them to make a point. An orchid was the centerpiece of a cascade bouquet."

Lynn's florist will evoke her marina country club/nautical wedding theme with table centerpieces of silver sailboat vases filled with white roses and small silver bowls holding floating white candles.

Daisies Do Tell—of Savings

Susan didn't have to spend a lot of money on her floral budget. "The area we're planning to be married in has so many beautiful flowers and plants. We'll use the grapevine wreath shaped like a heart and decorated with daisies and our names to show guests where the wedding is located. And, of course, I need a bouquet, my maid of honor needs one, and we have a flower girl."

 Fact

Seasonal weddings give you lots of ideas for inexpensive decorating. An added bonus is that many of the places you'll use for a ceremony or reception site will be decorated for the season, which translates into less decorating and less money on your end!

Susan decided on a bouquet of daisies accented with white and yellow roses. "Something exotic just wouldn't work with what I'm planning to wear," she said. "And the more exotic or out of season, the more expensive."

Since daisies are in season, Susan will likely get a bargain price on them—at the grocery store! "My aunt will put together white and yellow daisies and roses into simple bouquets for my maid of honor and me. And little baskets of daisies will serve as our reception-picnic centerpieces." The corsages and boutonnieres echo Susan's love for daisies as well.

 Essential

Investigate *www.blissezine.com*, a Web site with a floral guide that tells you types of flowers, their colors, and available seasons. It also helps to know the names of particular flowers and good substitutes for more expensive flowers than your budget will allow.

Decorating with Flowers

Kylie's florist is planning to use antique-style lace ribbon on the bridal bouquet and table arrangements. Kylie chose pale yellow roses for remembrance in her bouquet, but because these wouldn't match the colors worn by the mothers, she ordered white roses for them. Photos of the families of the bride and groom will be featured on the guestbook table.

Boutonnieres, Corsages, and Other Details

You need flowers for the setting of your wedding ceremony. If you're using a large church or synagogue, flower and ribbon decorations on the pews can really add up in cost. Decide whether you want to have a decoration on each pew, every other pew, or none at all. Figure out the cost differences between simple and elaborate choices, and then you'll know which you want.

Personal Flowers

Don't forget to budget for corsages for the mothers and grandmothers. Many brides order corsages with flowers similar to those in their bridal bouquets, but if you know your mother or your fiancé's mother loves a particular flower, you might want to incorporate it if it's not too expensive or out of season.

Be sure to find out whether any members of your wedding party have an allergy to certain flowers. You don't want to spend all that money and end up with them sneezing and red-eyed on this important day!

"When my mom found out we were ordering a silk corsage for my mother-in-law who's allergic to many flowers, she wanted one, too," said a recently married friend. "They look so pretty in little shadow boxes on the wall in their bedrooms."

Boutonnieres can be expensive if you get too fancy with the variety of flowers or with the arrangement. Most men generally prefer just a small, simple flower—one like those from the bride's bouquet—pinned to their lapel, anyway.

A Tisket, a Tasket

Kylie wanted a ring bearer, but thought that $35 was excessive for a ring pillow. "My aunt who loves to sew made one from a quarter of a yard of satin fabric she found marked down. She used some scraps of vintage lace she already had, and it was darling. It cost $4.98."

Susan found a similarly economical solution for the flower girl. "We found a white basket at Wal-Mart, hot-glued silk daisies around the rim, and filled it with silk rose petals for the flower girl," said Susan. "The cost? Under $10. The look was perfect for our outdoor wedding at the college."

Lynn doesn't want a ring bearer or a flower girl at the wedding. "We plan on having a nice reception dinner and lots of dancing. I don't think most of my friends would want to bring their children. Instead, it will be like a night out for them."

But a unity candle is something she's wanted as an extra touch at her wedding. "Everywhere we looked, they were so expensive. Just because I'm spending a lot on the wedding doesn't mean I want to waste money. What were we talking about—a pillar candle and some decoration?"

Instead, Lynn decided she'd try doing it herself. "I'm what you call 'craft-impaired'—all thumbs. But I figured if I messed up, I'd just lose a few dollars. I found something I could use at a craft store and then decorated it myself."

Remember that for your invitations and your flowers, as with everything else for your big day, setting your priorities is the first step in determining your budget. Be willing to spend money on what's most important and be more conservative with nonpriority items.

Invitation and Stationery Budget Worksheet

Stationery and postage

Save-the-date cards:	$_____
Invitations:	$_____
Thank-you cards:	$_____
Programs:	$_____
Postage:	$_____
Miscellaneous:	$_____

Other

_____:	$_____
_____:	$_____
_____:	$_____
_____:	$_____

Total: **$_____**

Floral Budget Worksheet

Flowers

Bridal bouquet:	$_____
Attendants' bouquets:	$_____
Flower girl's flowers:	$_____
Corsages and boutonnieres:	$_____
Ceremony site flowers and decorations:	$_____
Reception site flowers and decorations:	$_____

Miscellaneous flowers
and decorations: $_____
Miscellaneous: $_____

Other

_____: $_____
_____: $_____
_____: $_____
_____: $_____

Total: $_____

Chapter 9
Music and Transportation

Music delights the ear and adds an undeniably special touch to any occasion, especially so to a wedding. It sets the mood at the ceremony, whether the bride walks down the aisle to the familiar strains of Pachelbel's *Canon* or a more unconventional choice like Johnny Cash's *Ring of Fire*.

Ceremony Music

People might not remember the food they ate at a reception or what the flowers were, but they will remember the music they heard, danced to, and enjoyed. Most important, you and your fiancé need to agree on the type of music the two of you want at your wedding.

Do You Sing the Same Song?

Sometimes one person loves classical music and the other enjoys heavy metal. Well, that makes for some potentially interesting choices, especially on your wedding day. Consider the character of your ceremony and how the music will complement it. Whatever music you choose, it will be right for you, your fiancé, and your day together.

Make sure you check with your ceremony venue to find out what type of music they allow. In some locations, only taped music will be available or appropriate, but other places may require you to hire a live musician. If you are getting married in a religious setting, ask whether it's acceptable to stray from traditional pieces.

Hit the Right Key

Making sure you find the right musicians for the right price is the next important step in your budgeting. How important is music in your wedding? How much do you want to budget for it?

Susan and Nick, the college sweethearts with a modest budget, lucked out. "I started out thinking that it was going to be hard to have what we wanted with our budget," Susan said. "I mean, we just don't have that much to work with."

One day she was walking on campus, and it hit her: "There's a music department at our college and many of the music students hire out for occasions in the community. We have our choice of harpists, violinists, pianists, and organists—you name it! Even a steel band made up of students from the Bahamas!"

Susan and Nick had a long conversation and decided on a harpist. "I've always loved the music of a harp," Susan said. "And the setting seemed perfect for it. We'll seat her under a tree near the reflecting pool, and have her playing when the guests are gathering. Then she'll play during the ceremony and after, while we have our picnic. I can't imagine anything more elegant."

"Even better was the price," added Nick. "She gave us a special rate because we're students, and because she's living on campus."

 Fact

Although most musicians who play events have demo tapes or CDs, those don't give you any idea of how the musicians will sound live. To hear what they really sound like, ask whether you can drop in on an event they're playing before you make your commitment.

If you have a college or university in your area, even a small music school, you might be able to find musicians available there for your wedding and reception. Students are always in need of money for tuition and living expenses, and playing at a wedding gives them a chance to gain experience for their future careers.

Be sure to check the musicians' references and make certain that there is a backup plan in place if they are ill or can't make your event. Also offer to provide a reference for them if you're happy with their work.

Music in the Key of Life

A fan of the traditional, Kylie wants the church organist to play Wagner's *Bridal Chorus*. "I just always dreamed that I'd hear that music when I was walking down the aisle with my father. When I told Sean, he said he wanted me to have that," she said.

It took only a few minutes after church one Sunday to talk with the organist, find out whether he could play on the wedding date, and arrange payment details. Kylie was satisfied that the church organist will do a good job, since she had heard him play many Sundays and for a fellow church member's wedding. It may not be quite so easy for you to find ceremony musicians. Ask friends and family for recommendations. Your ceremony venue is also a good source of information.

Reception Music

Whether you opt for a live band, deejay, or your own iPod, your reception music will set the tone for the party. Your budget may determine which of these options you choose. Live bands are often the most expensive choice, and doing it yourself with an iPod and a pair of speakers is often the most economical, but there are issues to watch for with each option.

Finding a Band or Deejay

First, ask a friend or coworker whether she knows of a band or deejay or has seen either at a recent event. That's always a good way to find someone with ability and dependability. Deejays and bands advertise in the Yellow Pages, the newspaper, a local weekly shopper, on online bulletin boards, and on traditional posting boards at local businesses.

 Essential

The Web site *www.WeDJ.com* is a useful resource for finding a deejay for your wedding. Simply click on your state and county, and you'll find lists of deejays in your area. The site lets you easily contact deejays and set up arrangements.

Deejays are versatile and can accommodate a wide range of musical tastes and requests. Live bands tend to be less flexible, but they can specialize in everything from oldies covers to swing tunes.

Plan on making a number of calls and talking to several bands or deejays to find one that can meet your musical needs and fit your budget. At each interview, first make sure the band or deejay is available on your date, then ask how soon you need to commit. Ask whether you will be charged by the job or by the hour. If you are charged one flat fee, ask how many hours the band or deejay will be available for you. Find out whether the time frame you are quoted includes setup and cleanup. Finally, make sure the band or deejay's style fits your own. Request a musical collection list.

When you are ready to sign a contract, make sure there is a provision for what will happen if the band or deejay cannot make your event. Preferably, they will be able to guarantee that another band or deejay of similar ability will be at your event on time.

 Essential

Some couples choose to have the deejay act as master of ceremonies and announce them and their wedding party as they join the reception. If this is what you want, arrange it ahead of time. Give the deejay a list of the names and let him know how they're pronounced.

A Personal Touch

In Kylie and Sean's case, one deejay seemed particularly well suited to the job. The more they thought about the music, the more they knew they needed someone special. They wanted to honor their parents and grandparents, and they decided to do it with music.

This deejay said he would play Glenn Miller, Frank Sinatra, and the music that was popular when the couple's parents and grandparents were married. "Even though he was young, he knew all about the musical choices I wanted played for my parents and grandparents to dance to," said Kylie. "He'd played them for other events with older people. Yet he had some suggestions for modern music for us and guests our age. It felt like a match."

Alert

Give your band or deejay one list of must-play songs and a second list of songs they must not play under any circumstances. You'll hear your favorite tunes and the band or deejay will get a sense for the type of music you like and will be able to play similar music throughout the reception.

A Jazz Band

Lynn and John decided from the moment they started planning that they would be spending a big portion of their wedding budget on the reception. "We want a big dinner party for our friends," said Lynn. "John and I love jazz and go to clubs often." One night they went to a club and listened to their favorite group. John approached the musicians on break and asked whether they performed at weddings. He was given the name of their agent and contacted him.

"We were rather shocked at the price, but I talked with John and we agreed they were the group we wanted. We'll have them for fewer hours than a deejay, but it's worth the expense. After all, it's for our wedding day!"

An iPod Wedding

One bride decided she'd use her iPod and speakers for music at her reception after talking with other recent brides about their experiences using deejays. "I heard a few horror stories about deejays arriving late, demanding extra money, that sort of thing. But even the good ones wouldn't be careful about their selections. If a certain song is 'our song' and the correct version isn't brought to the reception, it's a disappointment. Besides, my fiancé really got into this aspect of the wedding. He worked on the music for months and made it so special for us. Our guests got a kick out of the high-tech aspect and we saved money, too!"

Make sure your iPod battery is fully charged before you get to the reception, and plug it in once you get there. Have a Plan B readily available in case your iPod fails you for any reason.

Hooking the iPod up to speakers at the reception is easy even for people not technically inclined, although there are a few caveats. Make sure your reception venue is set up to handle an iPod wedding. You may have to rent speakers that will work in the size of your venue. You can program your iPod ahead of time, but put a trusted friend or relative in charge of it. He can switch the music if the dance floor is too empty and prevent overenthusiastic guests from making unauthorized musical changes.

Get Me to the Church on Time!

Transportation to the church and reception contributes to the atmosphere of your day, whether you arrive in a limo or on a motorcycle. As soon as you booked your ceremony and reception sites, you probably determined what kind of wedding-day locomotion you need. If you require any special transportation other than your own two feet, arranging it can be enjoyable if you remember to use the same planning and budgetary concern you've applied to other elements of your wedding.

Renting a Limousine

Driving your own car or a family member's car may be the least expensive option for wedding-day transport, but many couples opt to rent a limousine to shuttle themselves and the wedding party around town.

Once again, consult your budget. Figure out how much money you have budgeted and how large a limousine you need. Limousine companies can accommodate any size wedding party, and you can even rent a motor coach or party bus to ferry all of your guests from Point A to Point B.

Check Things Out

Always get recommendations from friends, family, business associates, and your wedding vendors. Visit the company and talk to a representative about your needs and her prices, and ask to see her vehicles and a contract. Be sure to ask if any wedding packages are available and what they include.

Essential

> Try to have most details worked out before you draw up a contract arranging transportation for the wedding and reception. The more specific you can be about matters up front, such as times, tolls, number of people, and mileage, the fewer surprises you'll have later.

With more companies leasing their vehicles, it will be important to know who actually owns the limo. Who will be responsible if the transportation doesn't work as planned on your important day? Also, ask for proof of the limousine company's commercial livery insurance policy before you sign a contract.

Budgeting Details

Most limos are contracted at an hourly rate, which will quickly add up during the ceremony and reception. Find out exactly when the time clock begins; there can be a big difference between a company that charges as soon as its car leaves the garage and one that waits until it arrives at your house. Ask how many hours you will have the limousine and what happens if you go over your time. If you live in a large city, make sure you know who is responsible for paying tolls and parking charges. Make sure to budget for a gratuity, which can sometimes be as high as 20 percent. Be sure all these points are included in writing in your contract.

Make sure the contract specifies all information important to you, not just the name of the limo company. Include details such as what time you must be picked up and how many people will be riding in the vehicle. Also specify in the contract the exact type of car you need, so you aren't given something smaller than what you want or not as nice.

When a Limo's what You Want

Kylie hired a limousine to transport her and her wedding party to the church. "My parents and I want to go together—it will be very special, being with them just before I am married."

Lynn will ride to the marina country club in a limousine. After the reception, she and John will take the limo to the airport to catch their flight to Hawaii.

Limoless Choices

Limousines aren't the only mode of transportation available. There are plenty of ways to get your wedding party, your guests, and you to the reception in style.

 Essential

If you're serving alcoholic beverages at your reception, have a member of your wedding party stay alert for anyone who looks as if he or she needs a safe ride home. This is a duty the groom might ask his best man to unobtrusively perform.

Trolleys

City transportation companies sometimes lease local tourist trolleys. A driver wearing a period trolley-driver's uniform can pick up guests and take them on a scenic drive to their destination. The trip turns into an occasion of its own as riders enjoy the ambiance of this special ride. For a different look, consider renting antique cars or unusual vehicles such as Humvees.

Horse-Drawn Carriage

Kylie and Sean have decided to take a romantic horse-drawn carriage ride to their reception site, just a few blocks away from the church where they will be married. They felt this would make a nice transition from the ceremony to the celebration, while allowing them some private time together as newlyweds. Their contract includes a bottle of champagne and a tuxedoed driver.

Personal Cars

"We don't need a limo," said Susan, "but I don't want to crush my dress driving there in my little compact car. So I asked a college friend if he'd be willing to drive me in his big Lincoln and he was delighted to help. He wouldn't take any money; he said he enjoyed being asked to a picnic lunch outside on such a pretty day."

 Alert

Be mindful of the parking situation at your reception site. If your guests will have a difficult time finding the site or parking near it, consider chartering a bus to shuttle all guests from the wedding site. It's not just being careful— it's being courteous to your guests.

Specialty Transportation

Wedding transportation can be as different—and fun—as you want it to be. If it's a medieval wedding you have in mind, could you hire horses or a horse-drawn carriage? Couples have even taken hot-air balloons to their receptions. Your locale may provide you with unique transportation options.

A Watery Route

Not only is getting married along the water beautiful, it makes for an unforgettable way to get from the ceremony to the reception! You can rent private boats or ferries to take you from one shore to another.

Golf Carts

Many sites with sprawling outdoor acreage allow guests to rent golf carts. This is especially useful if you are getting married on one side of a property and holding your reception on the other and don't want Grandma Gertrude to fall into a gopher hole en route. Golf carts are also a quick and efficient way to transport the wedding party as you take pictures in different places.

Music and Transportation Budget Worksheet

Music

Ceremony site music:	$_____
Reception site music:	$_____
Tips/Gratuities	$_____
Total:	**$_____**

Transportation

Rental fee:	$_____
Additional vehicles:	$_____
Tips/Gratuities:	$_____
Miscellaneous:	$_____
Total:	**$_____**

Chapter 10
Picture This!

You want to capture memories from your wedding, but you don't want to throw away dollars on a picture of you tossing your bouquet. Rest easy. There is no shortage of photography packages, including nontraditional alternatives, to choose from. Evaluate your needs and wants, be creative, and decide on a photographer who fits your requirements. It *is* possible to choose the right photographer and get the photo album you want without sacrificing your budget.

Want Versus Need

Envision the final product. Will you have large keepsake albums with shots from your wedding and reception for yourself and your family, or will a small album and a few 5" × 7" photographs for your parents and wedding party serve your needs?

Size Matters

The package deal you make with your photographer can be as big or as small as you want. A friend or family member can take your photographs for free, or you can hire a team of photographers who will charge you thousands of dollars.

 Alert

Don't feel obliged to give away lots of wedding pictures to your family and friends. Share your photos on your wedding Web site or attach them to e-mails. If these aren't options, let your family and friends know how they can order copies from your photographer.

If a grand album of wedding photographs isn't a high-priority item in your wedding budget, then scale down the photography package. Ask the photographer to take fewer shots and develop fewer pictures. See whether it's possible for him to cover fewer hours than he normally would.

For a modest budget, choose a less ornate album and fewer posed shots that take a lot of time to compose.

Larger photography packages and complex shots increase the price. Photography packages differ in the number of hours covered, the number of shots taken, and the way your photos are delivered. You can order your photos à la carte, in an album, or in a coffee-table photo book.

 Essential

Some enterprising photographers offer discounts if you trust them to present the story of your wedding day the way they choose. You could end up with a storyboard or an unconventional album. This lets photographers experiment with new techniques and services that they might eventually offer in their regular packages.

Photographic Styles

Photographers have many different styles, and it's important to find one who will give you the photographs you want. Today's style is photojournalistic, without formal posed shots. The photographer captures the real emotional moments between the happy couple and their friends and family. These photos tell a natural, intimate story. Often, couples place these photos not in albums, but in white mats and simple, thin black frames and group a number of them on a wall in their home.

At the opposite side of the spectrum, formal photographers specialize in taking posed shots. These shots are easier to control, so you know what to expect from the photos. Posed shots give you a chance to be photographed with as many of your guests as you like.

You can also find a happy balance between photographic styles. You can have formal portraits with your family after the ceremony and candid shots of your friends at the reception. You also need to decide whether you want to use black-and-white, color, or sepia-toned film. Additionally, increasing numbers of photographers have gone digital, so think about whether you prefer film or digital cameras to document your wedding. You can mix and match styles and film to get the photography package that suits your needs.

Shop Around

Start your search for a photographer the same way you've gone about choosing other vendors, by getting recommendations from friends and family who have used a photographer recently. Look at their photographs and albums and ask questions about how the photographer worked out on that occasion. Here are a few sample questions:

1. Did the photographer show up on time?

2. Did the photographer dress appropriately?

3. Did the photographer bring enough film or disk memory for all the shots without having to scramble to get more?

4. Did the photographer capture all the important moments of the ceremony and the reception?

Identifying Candidates

Make sure the quality of photographs and the type of shots match what you are looking for. Ask your friends and family members whether they mind telling you what prices they paid for their wedding photography and whether proofs were delivered when expected. Listen carefully when you ask whether they felt pressure to buy more than they wanted or, say, whether they were unable to have a big group shot taken because the photographer insisted smaller groups would be better. Make sure the photographer did not tack on extra hidden fees or try to charge for services that weren't in the contract, such as touchups.

 Essential

Choosing to take fewer pictures does not mean you need to settle for a mediocre photographer. After all, these are important photographs that can't be taken again. Think about it this way: If there are minor mishaps that day, they probably won't be remembered. But a photograph is forever.

Check with your other vendors and your officiant. They may have worked at weddings and seen both good and not-so-good photographers. One bride recounted that her minister was very unhappy to hear she had chosen a certain photographer. At a previous wedding, the photographer had been late and held everyone up, and he'd taken shots at inappropriate times. The bridal couple later told the minister they'd been very unhappy with the photographer's work and his hard-sell approach. Fortunately, the bride-to-be hadn't yet put a deposit down and was able to make an agreement with a different photographer.

Cast a Wide Net

Look at photographers' Web sites to get a sense of their photographic style and how it fits with your vision for your wedding photographs. Online bridal forums often carry testimonials enabling previous brides to sound off on their wedding photographers. Just remember to take such comments with a grain of salt, since you don't know the posters or their situations.

You need not restrict yourself to professional photographers. If someone in your family wants to take photos and you like his work, accept his offer, though only if you truly believe he will do a great job. This occasion is too important to risk getting amateur-quality work.

Another alternative is to think locally. Many colleges and universities have photography departments or programs. You might be able to locate a skilled instructor or student who does weddings.

Speak with the Photographer

Once you have collected the names of a few photographers, make appointments with at least two of them to view their samples and get a sense of how they respond to your requests. Trust your gut. If your discussion is not what you expected, start looking elsewhere. You're not likely to become any happier with a person who doesn't make a good impression the first time around. Be sure you're comfortable with the person who will be with you, often in close quarters, for hours on your special day.

Here is a list of questions to ask your potential photographers:

1. Can we see samples of photography done at weddings like ours? What type of camera will you use? What type of shot do you consider your specialty?

2. What packages do you offer?

3. How much time will you spend working at our wedding? (Some photographers charge extra for overtime.)

4. Do you offer digital photography? (This saves money over traditional photography.)

5. Can we keep the negatives? If not, how long do we have to order pictures? Will the negatives be digital or film? When will our proofs be available?

6. Will photographs be available for our guests to purchase online?

7. How far ahead of the wedding date do we need to contract your time? (Bear in mind that during especially busy periods such as holidays and during the peak bridal months, photographers are booked far in advance.)

8. How much of a deposit is required? May we see a copy of the contract?

Be sure to ask the photographer how she will dress for your wedding. "I spent so much time and money trying to make sure that I had an elegant wedding," said one bride. "Then this photographer shows up in a polo shirt and khakis to take the wedding pictures. We were mortified!"

Ask whether the photographer does this work full-time, as a part-time occupation, or as a hobby. There's nothing wrong with part-time photographers, but be especially careful to check their references and portfolios.

Alert

Sometimes ritzy studios use the renowned name of one photographer but rely on a staff of unknowns. Ask to see your photographer's portfolio. You could be paying for a better photographer than you'll get. It's wise to double-check this so you know what to expect from your wedding photographs.

It's essential to determine that the person you interview is the one who will be your photographer later.

Developing a rapport with a photographer who turns out not to be yours can lead to disappointment if the quality of the product is less than you expected.

A Checklist of Posing Shots

Once you've picked your photographer, you should also discuss posing shots. Decide ahead of time which shots you want and when you want them taken. Point out those types of shots you particularly like, and be sure the photographer knows what kind you dislike.

Has the photographer taken shots similar to the type you want and in a location similar to your wedding site? You've carefully chosen your wedding and reception sites for a reason. If they're particularly beautiful or spiritual, you want that reflected in your photographs.

 Essential

Even if you are on a luxurious budget, don't go overboard with photography. Remember, it's your wedding, not a photo op! Don't spend too much time standing around having your picture taken. Your guests shouldn't be kept waiting for a long time while you have your photos taken.

A New Trend

Pre-wedding shots are a new trend. Some couples, eager to keep guests from sitting around while wedding-party shots are taken, prefer to have the photography done before the ceremony begins.

One bride thought she wouldn't like having her picture taken with her fiancé before the ceremony but changed her mind after she did it. "We had the chance to be with a very small number of people we loved and my fiancé and I got to see each other dressed for our wedding before anyone else did," she said. "It was so emotional for both of us. I'm glad we did it."

 Alert

Avoid potential embarrassment by alerting your photographer to any awkward situations. For instance, if your parents are divorced and not speaking to each other, the photographer shouldn't try to group them together in a shot with the bride and groom.

A Place to Start

Consider the following sampling of traditional photographs chosen by a bridal couple:

Portraits
- ❏ The bride
- ❏ The bride and groom
- ❏ The bride with her maid of honor and/or bridesmaids
- ❏ The groom with his best man and/or groomsmen
- ❏ The ring bearer and the flower girl
- ❏ The bride with her parents
- ❏ The groom with his parents

❏ The bride and groom with each set of parents
❏ The bride and groom with both sets of parents
❏ The entire wedding party

The Ceremony
❏ The ceremony site, outdoors and indoors (if applicable)
❏ Special guests and the parents of the bride and groom being seated by the groomsmen
❏ The groom walking down the aisle
❏ The groom, groomsmen, maid or matron of honor, and the bridesmaids waiting at the altar
❏ The flower girl and/or ring bearer walking down the aisle
❏ The bride walking down the aisle
❏ The wedding kiss
❏ The bride and groom leading the recessional
❏ Guests tossing birdseed or flower petals as the bride and groom leave the ceremony location

The Reception
❏ People signing the guest book
❏ The best man, maid of honor, parents, or others offering a toast
❏ The bride and groom as they listen to the toasts
❏ Pictures of the guests seated at the tables
❏ The bride and groom's first dance
❏ The bride and her father dancing
❏ The groom and his mother dancing
❏ The cake

- ❏ The bride and groom as they cut the cake
- ❏ The bride and groom as they leave the reception site

Behind the Scenes

- ❏ The bride and groom as they get dressed, with or without their attendants or parents
- ❏ The bride pinning on her father's boutonniere
- ❏ The mother helping the bride with her dress or veil
- ❏ The bride and groom as they leave for the ceremony

Essential

If photographs of the wedding party are being taken before the ceremony, ask the photographer to catch that first moment when the bride and groom see each other. Some couples consider the two close-up shots the most memorable ones, and you will probably want them no matter what size the wedding-photograph package is.

Candid Shots

In looking through either the photographer's portfolio or albums or proofs of recently married friends, you may notice that the candid shots capture more than posed portraits. Although it's always good to plan what you want, if you have the right photographer, you should be able to trust his judgment.

Even if you've decided on a formal photography package, let your photographer know that if she sees a really great casual shot, it's OK to snap it. Sometimes casual shots end up being the most memorable ones. That candid photo of the four-year-old flower girl gazing enraptured at the wedding cake or your grandparents dancing check-to-cheek just might say it all.

Some Alternatives

There are good reasons for not having a photographer at your wedding. Some couples have a small, intimate wedding with just a few family members and friends and don't want the intrusion of an outsider on their special day. Others can't find a photographer within their limited budget. Still others are simply uncomfortable with photographers popping up here and there and snapping shots.

A nice alternative is to have a portrait taken in a studio. The shots for these are done in a controlled setting with particularly good lighting and without the weather and time constraints of ceremony and reception settings. There are just the three of you—bride, groom, and photographer; no one else sees or hears how the shots are set up.

Special moments between the bride and groom as they gaze at each other, for instance, can be very intimate; neither needs to feel pressured by onlookers. If either of you has ever been unhappy with the way posed or candid shots have turned out—"Oh, no, I don't look like that, do I?"—then a studio portrait can be a great alternative.

Your Guests Can Take Great Shots, Too!

Another good alternative is to hand out disposable cameras to a number of people at the ceremony and reception. Perhaps they'll take special shots that the professional photographer misses. They can capture moments at the wedding that are particularly meaningful to them. Do put a cautionary note on the cameras if your church or synagogue does not want photos taken during the exchange of vows.

 Fact

Instead of having a guest book, one couple had a favorite picture of themselves blown up and mounted on poster board. It sat on a table at the wedding, where guests signed around the picture. The couple had it mounted and framed so they could hang it in their first home.

Having your guests do informal photography can also help you save money. Some couples have a professional photographer for the ceremony and use the informal shots guests take at the reception for their album. The choice is yours!

From a Kid's Point of View

Older children enjoy using inexpensive disposable cameras to record a child's-eye view of the wedding and reception. These pictures, while not always of the quality of those taken by adults, can be charming and will give children the opportunity to be part of things. Later, you can put the photos into frames and present them as gifts.

Getting It on Video

Having a videographer document your wedding gives you another visual way to remember your wedding day. It's a fad that became a trend, and now more couples are adding this service to their wedding. As video cameras become more popular and are priced more affordably, more people have started recording their own special events.

And the Oscar Goes to . . .

Of course, wedding videos run the gamut from choppy homemade productions to master works of art worthy of an Academy Award. Prices vary widely as well, ranging from hundreds of dollars to thousands. With this kind of expenditure, it's important to look carefully for a good videographer, especially since many couples want their videographer to be just as good in quality as their photographer.

Gather recommendations from the same people you ask about photographers. In addition, you can ask your photographer to recommend a videographer, because the two often work together.

Choosing a Videographer

Many of the interview questions you ask of your photographer also pertain to a videographer. Ask to see a sample of the prospective videographer's work. Find out what kind of equipment he will bring to the wedding, whether sound will be recorded, and whether he will edit the video. Will you be able to copy the video?

 Question?

What are the benefits of videotaping our wedding?
The video that a videographer produces allows you to watch your wedding and reception again and again to relive that special day. If friends or family are unable to come to the wedding, a video is a vivid way to show them the event.

Beware of well-intentioned but inexperienced family members who have just bought a new videotape recorder and can't wait to use it. Sure, they can bring it to the wedding and make a video for themselves, but do you really want to rely on Uncle Joe for your wedding video? Only you know the answer to that question.

Uncle Joe may not have professional training, but what about that friend who graduated from film school and can't wait to be the next Hitchcock or Scorsese? Ask yourself the chances that your wedding video will look like a scene from *Rear Window* or *The Departed*. If the answer is something you can live with, go for it.

No matter whom you ask to perform videography duties at your wedding, make sure the quality of the video will be as good as a professional job. If so, then you have your videographer, possibly for the price of the videotape.

Three Possible Scenarios

Susan and Nick found a student photographer who does weddings on the weekends, but they decided that a video wasn't for them. "It just felt like too much for such a small outdoor wedding."

Lynn and John have opted for a video of their wedding. They found a photographer and a videographer based on the recommendation of friends who'd been married recently. "We think it'll be wonderful to have a video to look at later."

 Essential

Maybe you want a video of your wedding day but you just don't have the money or a friend or relative who can do the job. Think about having just the ceremony videotaped. For many couples, that's the most important part of the day anyway.

Kylie and Sean shopped carefully for their photographer, but decided against a videographer, preferring to spend the money on the band that is to be featured at their reception.

The Visuals Budget Worksheet

Use this handy worksheet to document expenses for your wedding. Keeping track of everything you spend will ensure that you stay within your budget. You might want to make a copy of the worksheet and tuck it into your purse or daily calendar so you remember to make entries as soon as you make the purchases. You might need to customize this worksheet a bit depending on your particular wedding plans.

Photography package:	$_____
Extra photos:	$_____
Potential add-ons	$_____
Videography package:	$_____
Tips/Gratuities:	$_____
Miscellaneous:	$_____
Total:	**$_____**

Chapter 11
Remember the Extras

It's the little touches that people remember, the extras you offer your wedding guests to let them know you're glad they've come to help you celebrate. But the little things add up and can break your budget, so take the advice of that old maxim: Watch the pennies and the dollars will take care of themselves.

Wedding Favors and Frills

In medieval times, knots made of ribbon were attached to a bride's dress and torn off by guests in a spirited contest for a trophy. In Victorian England, ribbons were tied around charms, which were then baked into the wedding cake. Bridesmaids pulled the charms out of the cake, each of which was supposed to tell the bridesmaid's future. For example, the bridesmaid who pulled a flower could expect love to bloom in her life.

Wedding favors add a warm touch to a wedding reception. Many couples like to give a small, heartfelt gift for their guests to take home as a memento of the wedding. Sometimes the favors serve double duty as a decorative touch on a reception table, such as silver frames that double as place-card holders.

Favors for Your Budget

Favors can be as small as a little bag of candy or as big as—well, as big as your budget allows. They can be as inexpensive as a votive candle or as pricey as a sterling Tiffany bud vase engraved with the couple's names and the date of the wedding. It's up to you, in light of your budget, to decide what to do.

Once you decide, stay firm with your choice. It's all too easy to add this and that because you don't feel like you're spending much, until suddenly you've spent three times what you budgeted.

If your budget is strained, it is acceptable to skip the favors altogether. Ultimately, your guests attend your wedding to share your joy, not to collect a matchbook with your name on it. That being said, favors are a polite way to thank your guests for going out of their way to come to your wedding. There are many inexpensive wedding favors your guests will enjoy.

Old Favorites

Some favors remain popular year after year. Small candles make a lovely gift that can be as inexpensive or expensive as you wish. Wrap one in a circle of tulle and tie it with ribbon.

You can purchase supplies at craft stores, discount stores, party stores, and on the Internet. Check to see whether you can get a discount for buying candles in bulk from stores or Web sites.

 Essential

You can place your favors in a decorated basket at the reception so that guests may take them as they leave for home. If you're having a sit-down dinner, you can put a favor at each place setting.

So Many Ideas

Just mention the phrase "wedding favors," and everyone you meet has a suggestion. The Internet is also full of suggestions and Web sites that offer merchandise at competitive prices. Message boards are another good source of inspiring ideas.

Don't feel you have to outdo the last wedding you went to with your favors. If you're creative and have the time, make something that only you can do. No time or all thumbs at crafts? You'll find plenty of ideas for favors that come ready-made.

One bride read online about a celebrity wedding in which guests were given little silver bells to ring as the newly wedded couple left the church. She found bells available on a Web site and bought them in bulk at a discounted price. Another bride found a company that sold ribbon streamers to throw at the bridal couple, which turned out to be a hit at her wedding.

The selection of candy favors is endless. There are companies that make chocolate candy wrappers printed with whatever message you wish. Another way of personalizing candies is to order lollipops decorated with a bride and groom or have the bride and groom's names printed on the lollipop wrappers. A bride searching for favors for what she termed her Cinderella wedding found a suggestion for chocolate mice made of Hershey's kisses that looked darling on her reception tables.

Eco-weddings are becoming more popular, and couples can give tiny tree seedlings and know that something from their day will grow in the years to come. Flower seeds are also popular favors. Some companies print the names of the bride and groom and their wedding date on packets of seeds. When the seeds sprout, your guests can enjoy pretty blooms and remember the day you were married. Another unusual offering is butterflies, which guests can take home and release into their gardens.

Make Your Own Favors

Making your own favors can save you money and add a special personalized touch to your wedding day. This task doesn't have to be a solitary endeavor. You can enlist your fiancé or a few friends and make a party out of assembling favors.

 Essential

Use your imagination to come up with one-of-a-kind wedding favors that mean something special to both you and your fiancé. Make potpourri that smells like the first bouquet your fiancé bought for you.

Heavenly Scents

Potpourri wrapped in tulle or placed in little boxes or sachets can be a sweet-smelling favor for guests to take home and enjoy for months to come. You can choose from many scents and spend just a few dollars a bag. You can make your own potpourri from flower petals found in your own garden and some scented oils.

Decorative soaps are a welcome gift that cost only a little time and effort to make. Molds and materials are available in most craft stores. Or find a pretty pastel soap or two, wrap it in tulle, and tie this with a ribbon and maybe a silk flower for a thoughtful wedding favor.

Creative Candles

You can use a gold or silver craft pen to inscribe your names or initials and the date of the wedding on inexpensive votive candleholders or wine glasses. There are also kits for making faux engravings. A design of dots, scrolls, or a line from a poem adds a creative touch.

A scented votive candle becomes a simple but lovely favor when placed in a little glass holder and wrapped with tissue or tulle and tied with ribbon. Later, when guests burn the candle, they'll remember your wedding.

Inexpensive champagne glasses filled with the new scented gel-candle wax make beautiful wedding favors. Tint the gel until it turns the color of champagne, pour it into glasses, then stir to create air bubbles that look like champagne bubbles. Insert wicks and you have candles that look like glasses of bubbly. They're perfect as decorations on the reception tables, and guests will love to take them home.

Candies and Chocolates

The easiest wedding favor to make is a candy favor— and just to be clear, you're not making the candy yourself!

Present your guests with a handful of colorful mints or foil-wrapped chocolates.

Jordan almonds are perennial wedding favorites. They come in white, pastels, black, and even silver and gold foil-wrapped white almonds. Almonds are a symbol of life, and the sugared coating a wish that bride and groom have more sweetness than bitterness in their lives together.

 Fact

A charming candy-favor idea is to wrap five almonds in a tulle circle, twist, and tie a ribbon around the bundle. The number is symbolic, representing health, wealth, happiness, fertility, and longevity.

Hershey's kisses and hugs are always popular. Simply wrap a few chocolates in tulle or place them in a little favor box. Favor boxes come in more shapes and sizes and prices than you can imagine.

Wedding Party Gifts

They've been there for you through good times and bad. If you're the bride, they've gone with you to find the perfect dress and shoes and graciously helped to make this wedding possible. If you're the groom, they've been your buddies when you needed someone to listen, and maybe they helped you find a tux that saved you from looking like a refugee from a high school prom.

 **Essential**

Wedding gifts for attendants fall into two categories: those they can use on the day of the wedding and those that are everyday, useful items. Deciding on the category is as important as how much you spend.

They're your wedding party. And you want to find something special to thank them for all they've already done and will be doing on your wedding day. As with other purchases for your wedding, you need to decide how much you can spend. Remember that the care with which you choose their gifts will mean more to your attendants than actual money spent.

For Female Attendants

Gifts your bridesmaids can use at the wedding include jewelry, handbags, dressy headbands, and cashmere wraps or chiffon stoles.

For jewelry, you can choose a style of earrings or necklaces (or both) that matches the bridesmaid gowns. Make sure to accommodate bridesmaids who don't have pierced ears. Bracelets are a little trickier to buy because wrist sizes vary. If you want your bridesmaids to enjoy your gift on an everyday basis, look for jewelry that can be worn with work clothes or casual dress.

Thoughtful everyday gifts include baskets filled with items for pampering, such as aromatherapy candles, foaming bath salts, fancy bath sponges, manicure sets, a novel to read in the tub, and after-bath body lotion. You can buy ready-made packages or assemble them yourself by choosing items that fit your budget.

Alert

To avoid stoking any gift envy, buy similar items for all members of the wedding party. Spend an equivalent amount on the bridesmaids and groomsmen, then set aside something extra for your honor attendants.

A vase is a practical gift that can be used to hold blossoms either at home or the office. Personalize it with a gold or silver craft pen or use a kit to do faux engraving on the glass. A little frame with a picture of your attendant and you is a nice present from one friend to another. Or you can give small, memorable photo albums.

For Male Attendants

Groomsmen can get some use on the day of the wedding out of a set of cuff links. However, a new tie might be a better choice if you want the recipient to wear it more often. A men's manicure set or small travel bag is also a handy gift. Alcohol-themed gifts like beer-can holders, drinking glasses, pub signs, and flasks are other popular choices.

Essential

Many places that specialize in gifts for wedding attendants offer discounts if you order items in bulk. This is worth considering if you are buying the same gifts for everyone in your entire wedding party.

For Any Attendant

Gift certificates to the local gym, CDs of the wedding and reception music, fancy pen-and-pencil sets, business-card holders, appointment calendars, address books, fancy travel mugs, even a silver-plated computer mouse all make useful gifts.

Then There's Mom and Dad and . . .

Sometimes the bride and groom buy gifts for their parents and grandparents. A number of companies offer monogrammed handkerchiefs for men and women. You can order double silver frames engraved with "Daddy's Little Girl" to hold a picture of you as a little girl on one side and as a young woman on your wedding day on the other. Handsomely framed pictures of bride or groom with parents or grandparents are always priceless gifts.

DIY Centerpieces

If you like the idea of giving your reception tables a personalized touch, think about making your own centerpieces. It can be great fun and save you money as well.

Do-it-yourself centerpieces are becoming more popular these days as brides look for ways to set their receptions apart.

Take the Plunge

"I wanted to have something different at my reception," Tess, a new bride, said recently. "It seemed I was seeing so many stiff, formal centerpieces at wedding receptions I attended. There was one reception where the florist had made these huge centerpieces and totally forgotten that people would want to see each other and talk to each other across the table. And when I started planning my wedding and looked at the prices—well, I couldn't believe it. So I decided to try making a centerpiece myself and it turned out just fine."

 Alert

Wholesale outlets like Costco sell flowers in bulk at a discount. You can order live flowers ahead of time and pick them up before your wedding. You can rent or buy inexpensive vases or bowls and assemble your centerpieces yourself.

Tess found silk flowers that were a perfect imitation of her real bouquet flowers and used glass containers she found at the dollar store. "You just put some floral foam you find at the store to the bottom of the container and stick the flowers in until they look right," she reported, admitting that while she shopped one day she watched an employee at a silk flower store put together such an arrangement. "She made it look so easy, and it was." As a precaution in case her own work didn't measure up, Tess wrote down the price a ready-made arrangement would cost. "Turns out I didn't need outside help!"

Some Easy Real Blooms

Sometimes simple is best. Try filling glass vases with a dozen or two fresh blooms and set them in the middle of the tables. Each table doesn't have to match—it might be more fun to place a dozen tulips on one table, a dozen daffodils on the next, and so on for a spring wedding. Or group several vases of different blooms on the same table.

Go for Something Different

A new trend is to fill a vase or glass container with fruit such as lemons or limes before inserting flowers. The use of ornamental branches or grasses can be striking. Grouping fall fruits and vegetables makes an appealing seasonal theme. If you're getting married near Christmas, go with stylish little trees on your table or figurines that spotlight the season.

Essential

> Edible centerpieces are wonderfully tempting for guests. Apples in the fall and oranges in the summer are beautiful and tasty—just let your guests know they can eat the centerpieces if the urge strikes them. Send your guests home with the leftovers.

Whatever the season, have lots of candles, little votives, or tea lights. Candlelight is wonderfully flattering and an inexpensive way of creating a luxe look. Check with your reception site to see whether there are any restrictions on candlelight before proceeding with your plans.

You can also group your favors as a centerpiece. Candy favors, even candy bars, are a popular feature at weddings today. Fill inexpensive glass-lidded jars with a variety of colorful candies, provide ladles and containers, and let guests scoop out their own candy. They can consume the candy right at the reception.

The Extras Budget Worksheet

Use this handy worksheet to document expenses for your wedding. Keeping track of everything you spend will ensure that you stay within your budget. You might want to make a copy of the worksheet and tuck it into your purse or daily calendar so you remember to make entries as soon as you make the purchases. You might need to customize this worksheet a bit, depending on your particular wedding plans.

Favors: $_____
Wedding-party gifts: $_____
Miscellaneous: $_____

Other Expenses:

_____ : $_____
_____ : $_____
_____ : $_____
_____ : $_____
Total: $_____

Chapter 12
Budgeting for the Unexpected

Unexpected expenses will inevitably arise. Something you hadn't planned on suddenly must be factored into a budget you thought was set. Now what? Advance budgeting for the unexpected in both time and money ensures that you can handle anything. Whether dealing with small snafus or large-scale disaster, here are some strategies that can help protect your bank account and your sanity.

The Real Budget Busters

Miscellaneous expenses can comprise anywhere from 2 to 12 percent of a wedding budget, depending on your working definition of "miscellaneous." Under this category fall all those little charges ($60 here and another $30 there) that you haven't factored into major budget expenses. They usually aren't altogether unexpected, though too often couples do not seriously consider miscellaneous expenses until they start to add up. Five percent of a total wedding budget of $20,000 is a hefty $1,000. You and your fiancé might not have even thought about setting that much aside for "trivial" expenses.

Tell Me what They Are

The nice thing about miscellaneous expenses is that you can actually plan for them. Here's a partial list of miscellaneous expenses:

1. Marriage-license fees

2. Blood tests required in your state

3. Emergency supplies like a first-aid kit and extra pantyhose for the wedding day

4. Favors

5. Tips and gratuities

6. Transportation expenses related to wedding errands

Budget for any unique circumstances. For instance, if you live far away from where you will be married, factor in the airfare for multiple visits to the wedding site to meet with vendors and plan your event. Decide whether you and your fiancé will buy new clothes and accessories for the honeymoon or any pre-wedding festivities. The same goes for primping in the days and weeks before the wedding. You may want to indulge in a spa treatment, but make sure it's in the budget before you book it. Beauty products often slip into the budget unnoticed. Account for everything from teeth-whitening products to extra tubes of lip gloss. This might seem nit-picky, but keeping track of everything can prevent you from dealing with budget shortfalls.

Come Up with a Plan

One way to lighten the load of miscellaneous expenses is to sit down with your fiancé and agree on how much is a significant amount, say $50. This means that each of you may spend up to $50 on wedding-related expenses without mention, but for anything over that you must record the amount. A budget can withstand a few $10 expenditures without a lot of stress, but if each of you is spending $100 here and there the budget can easily get out of control.

One couple using a wedding checking account ran into trouble because they didn't sit down and balance the checkbook together. "We nearly bounced a check because he paid for something and didn't write it down," said Dawn. "Then I wrote a big check and just happened to think to talk to him about it. We looked at each other and then grabbed the checkbook to figure things out and see if we had enough money to cover everything until we made another deposit!"

Question?

What do you consider a "miscellaneous" expense?
Discuss this question with your fiancé. It's an important way to understand spending styles. If one of you thinks numerous small expenses are no big deal and the other does, it's a big deal that needs to be discussed!

Changing Course

Sometimes you can overdraw your miscellaneous budget with a last-minute change of plans. If you're planning something that can be iffy, like having an outdoor wedding in a season with unpredictable showers, you have to provide an alternate arrangement. This could involve miscellaneous expenses.

Some couples decide to rent a tent, then realize they didn't include this expense under the original reception-venue expense. Their solution is to stick the cost under miscellaneous expenses, so that suddenly there's a big blip in that category. Remember that the additional money has to come from somewhere in your budget, and you may need to decrease spending in other areas to account for the miscellaneous increase.

Is It Time for Help?

A bridal consultant can be a big help in stemming a tide of miscellaneous expenses. A person with years of experience in planning weddings will be able to warn you about unforeseen budgetary pitfalls. A bridal consultant might be able to help you with financial planning on a short-term basis if you want to avoid hiring someone for a large fee.

Tips and Fees

It's prudent to thank all of the people who worked hard and dedicated their time to making your wedding such a memorable experience with a monetary tip. Keep track of tips carefully! Some gratuities may be built into your contract, especially for duties such as catering, and tipping some vendors may not be necessary.

Wedding Officiant

If the officiant of your wedding ceremony is a member of the clergy, find out the fee you're expected to pay. Don't assume that officiating at your wedding is part of her salary. Weddings are not considered part of regular duties, meaning the officiant should be compensated. If the officiant doesn't want to name a figure, ask some friends or family members who have been recently married what they paid. Think about what an important role this person is performing for you. If a fee is not accepted, then make an appropriate donation to the church or synagogue.

Civil officials who perform a wedding might not be allowed to charge for their services. Check before the wedding to see whether there is a fee and how much it is.

A Tip to the Wise

The general rule for tipping is 10 to 15 percent of the total charge and up to 20 percent if the service is exceptional. *Do* tip the following vendors:

- **Caterers, wait staff, and bartenders.** Check your contract. Gratuities may be included, but make sure they cover the entire staff. If they don't, decide on a flat dollar amount for each member of the wait staff.
- **Delivery people.** You do not need to tip the florist or the baker, but you should tip the people who deliver the finished products in one piece to the reception site.
- **Photographer and videographer.** Use your discretion. Photographers and videographers don't always expect a tip, but this is a nice way to thank the people who develop your priceless images.

- **Deejays and band members.** This is up to you. If the deejay has a partner or there are multiple band members, figure a flat rate per person and deliver the tip to the leader.
- **Limousine driver.** A gratuity may be built into your contract, so check before you hand out the cash.
- **Parking and coatroom attendants.** These helpers should receive $1 per car or coat.
- **Makeup artists and hair stylists.** You normally leave a tip when you get your hair cut, so a hairdo for your wedding requires an even greater tip.
- **Wedding coordinator.** Say thank you to the person who introduced you to all of the other vendors.

If you find that certain vendors for your wedding provide excellent service, consider writing them a note or offering a recommendation or reference. Some vendors also have a section for testimonials on their Web sites. It's nice for a professional to be appreciated, and it's doubly nice when hard work pays off in future business.

Planning for Special Needs

Your wedding day is a special occasion for everyone involved. You should anticipate your guests' needs so that everyone has an enjoyable time at your wedding.

Hearing-Impaired Guests

If someone at your wedding is hearing-impaired, think about hiring an interpreter. That way everyone will "hear" you say your vows, even understand every embarrassing detail of every toast. At a recent wedding, several guests reported that seeing the words of a ceremony translated into sign language was a wedding highlight, and they were not hearing-impaired. "There was something very beautiful about someone quietly interpreting the words with their hands," one guest said.

 Fact

Most public buildings conform to federal and state laws that require accessibility for handicapped people, but pay particular attention to the specific needs of friends and family attending your wedding and reception. You want to give them a good time, not cause them problems.

Contact your local interpreting agency or deaf and hard-of-hearing community association for names of interpreters you can hire for your occasion. Someone in your circle of friends and family may be able to serve as an interpreter, especially if the hearing-impaired person is a family member.

Physically Disabled Guests

If you have a family member or friend who is disabled and will have a difficult time getting around at the wedding and reception sites, consider asking a member of the wedding party or another person you know well to be available to help. Consider arranging special transportation, especially if the person will not be able to attend the wedding without it.

Special Dietary Requirements

Find out whether any of your guests have special dietary needs, restrictions, or allergies. Be very careful to honor their requests for substitutions or special arrangements when planning your food and drink.

 Question?

What if any of our guests are vegetarian?
Even if there aren't any strict vegetarians at your gathering, people might not eat a particular type of meat and will appreciate your thinking of them. Children who attend will also appreciate having something they like to eat and drink.

Be sure to tell your caterer of any special dietary needs well in advance of your wedding, which might entail more work than you realize. Ask whether there is an additional charge for special requests, and specify any such arrangements in your food-and-drink package agreement.

Wedding Insurance 101

You don't want to think about it, but it has to be said. Things happen. That's why many couples consider wedding insurance. A wedding is actually one of the biggest investments you will ever make; many couples spend more on their wedding than they would for an automobile or a trip abroad. Logically, then, wedding insurance might be a good idea.

You've been charging everything on a credit card so that you have recourse in case anything happens, and you've signed contracts putting every agreement about goods and services in writing—and that's great. However, those steps won't get your money back if something unforeseen happens.

Imagine the worst-case scenario: Your wedding and reception have to be cancelled because one of you falls ill; your wedding gown or his custom-made tuxedo is lost or damaged; a hurricane or other bad weather requires you to postpone the wedding; one of you is called up for active duty; a vendor doesn't supply your wedding cake; the wedding rings are lost or damaged—any number of things could go wrong. Now imagine that you are financially protected in the event that one of these things disrupts your wedding day.

If you're having the wedding and reception at a private home, you might want to get insurance in case someone is injured or there is damage to property. Although a homeowner insurance policy may cover such incidents, it's best not to file a claim against it if you don't have to. Some reception sites require you to carry wedding insurance, so make sure you investigate this if you haven't already.

Contact your insurance agent for quotes or look up wedding insurance companies on the Internet. You'll have to decide if it's worth the extra money (possibly a few hundred dollars for a five-figure wedding), and you'll need to include the cost of protecting your investment in your budget. The more you spend on your wedding, the better idea wedding insurance may be.

If Something Goes Seriously Wrong

The likelihood is that any mishaps that occur will not threaten your wedding day, and chances are you will be the only one who notices them. There are worse things that can happen than to have a particular arrangement for your wedding go awry.

However, serious situations do arise. Step back, take a deep breath, assess, and then decide on a plan of action. Above all, don't panic.

 Essential

There is only so much you can do to plan for the unexpected. If your wedding plans are seriously disrupted for any reason, experiencing a period of grief is natural. You have anticipated and planned for this event for months, so it is natural to mourn if your wedding does not happen.

Don't despair. Try to find anything positive in the situation. To start, you have your fiancé. Without your better half, there would *really* be no wedding. Work together to find a solution. You've got that wedding insurance, right? Depending on the plan you chose, you could be covered for any unforeseen circumstances and delinquent vendors.

If you're facing a financial crunch, downsize your planning and expenses. Immediately. If others don't understand, that's too bad. It's not the time to hide from reality and have more financial stress than you need right now.

If an unexpected military deployment disrupts your romantic plans, see if the two of you can plan a faster, smaller ceremony if you don't want to wait until later. Do what's best for the two of you. You might even consider eloping and having a quick honeymoon! You can always have a party to celebrate later.

If a friend or family member dies, then you and your fiancé alone know whether that person would want you to go forward with your wedding. Do what your hearts tell you.

When Vendors and Venues Let You Down

Perhaps one of your vendors lets you down. The bakery that was supposed to bake your wedding cake goes out of business. Your wedding dress arrives without the matching jacket for your winter wedding. The reception site apologizes for an accidental double booking and shows you the door.

Check the Fine Print

In such a situation, the first thing you should do is check your contract. Keep all of your wedding agreements and contracts handy in a three-ring binder so if you run into a problem, you aren't frantically sifting through paperwork to find what you need. If a delivery can't be made, examine your recourse for having your deposit returned.

The Next Step

Nicely but firmly tell the delinquent vendor you will contact your local Better Business Bureau if he shirks his financial responsibility. Write letters. Make yourself a burr in his side if he thinks he can just apologize and walk away from a mess.

 Alert

Most attorneys will tell you they're able to resolve many contractual disputes without expensive litigation or court appearances. Their jobs are first to seek a resolution that avoids formal legal proceedings. Let your attorney handle any serious complaint you have with a vendor.

If you have a significant dispute on your hands, for instance if you've paid a large deposit for a service that a vendor is suddenly refusing to return, contact an attorney. The fee will be worth the legal assistance.

Guess Who's Coming to Dinner

So friends and relatives you haven't seen in a long time decide at the last minute to show up for your happy day— even though you weren't expecting them because they didn't send in their R.S.V.P. cards on time.

If you are having a buffet at your reception, the caterer will have allowed for unexpected guests. If your head count is higher than what you expected for a sit-down dinner, ask your caterer or reception-site manager how to work out the difference.

Stay calm. Offer them the same information on lodging you've made available for all guests. Do not, under any circumstances, break your budget to accommodate expenses for unexpected guests. Do not let them guilt you into paying for accommodations or hosting them yourself.

Some people accommodate unexpected guests by offering guest rooms, a sofa bed, or an inflatable mattress. If you do decide to have guests in your space, know that it may be an additional expense for food and other items, and it's company you may feel you have to entertain at a stressful time.

When Borrowing Is a Good Idea

Uh oh. You don't have enough money for the wedding. Whatever the reason, you don't want to downsize your wedding or elope. You need funds, and you need them sooner rather than later. Borrowing a lot of money or running up credit card charges to pay for a wedding is not behavior we advise. However, if your money crunch is a temporary situation or you don't need to borrow much, you might think about a loan.

Essential

> All the challenges you may face in pulling off your wedding will help you learn how to work together as a team with your fiancé. It's great practice for life as a married couple—and that's worth everything, all the tears and the laughter and the heated discussions.

Keep It In the Family

Turning to family first is the best idea, unless those are the same people who caused the problem to begin with by taking back a promise of financial help. These loans don't require credit approval or have interest charges and payment dates that aren't subject to change. Offer to sign a note for the money with the terms for repayment clearly stated, and make certain you intend to honor your commitment, not act like it's going to be a gift.

Turn to a Financial Institution

If you have to borrow money from a financial institution, see whether you can take out a loan using your savings or CD account as collateral. The collateral must stay in the bank or credit union until you repay the loan. If you don't have a savings account, a local bank or credit union might still approve a loan for you.

Essential

Check your credit rating before you apply for a loan. Your credit rating determines how much money you are eligible to borrow. Although basic reports are free, you can purchase a more detailed report for a small fee.

Credit Cards

Avoid overcharging your credit cards. When all else fails, however, use a credit card with the lowest interest rate you can find. Check on whether taking out a cash advance carries a lower interest rate, and use that option first if you can.

The How Much Have You Gone Over? Budget Worksheet

Use this handy worksheet to document expenses for your wedding. Keeping track of everything you spend will ensure that you stay within your budget. You might want to make a copy of the worksheet and tuck it into your purse or daily calendar so you remember to make entries as soon as you make the purchases. You might need to customize this worksheet a bit, depending on your particular wedding plans.

Miscellaneous Expenses

Marriage-license fees: $_____
Blood tests: $_____

Emergency supplies: $_____

Favors: $_____

Wedding insurance: $_____

Tips and gratuities: $_____

Extra transportation

Expenses: $_____

_____ : $_____

_____ : $_____

_____ : $_____

_____ : $_____

_____ : $_____

_____ : $_____

Special Needs   **$_____**

Unexpected Expenses

_____ : $_____

_____ : $_____

_____ : $_____

Total miscellaneous expenses: $_____

Amount over budget: $_____

Expenses put on credit card/

loans taken out: $_____

Total: **$_____**

Chapter 13
Guests' and Attendants' Budgets

You've been thinking about the budget for your wedding and reception, and that's been quite enough work, right? Not so fast! While you're watching your budget, it's also important to look out for the budgets of your guests and attendants. They are spending hundreds or even thousands of dollars in transportation, lodging, clothing, and gifts so they can be there for your special day. They will appreciate any help you can give them in alleviating some of these costs.

The Wedding Party

The biggest way to reduce your own expenses relating to the wedding party is to limit the number of attendants. While you want to have your friends who have been near and dear to you as your attendants, remember that you are including them by inviting them to your ceremony. Every groomsman needs a boutonnière, every bridesmaid needs a bouquet, and they all need thank-you gifts. But keep in mind that you aren't the only one spending money on your wedding day.

Attending You Can Be Expensive

The financial cost of being an attendant can be steep. Your maid of honor and bridesmaids have to pay for their dresses and any necessary alterations, jewelry and accessories, dress shoes, hair and makeup charges, special undergarments, travel expenses, bachelorette-party expenses, and shower and wedding presents.

The groomsmen have it easier. They pay for the rental of their tuxes, dress shoes, maybe some dark socks, bachelor-party expenses, and a wedding gift. As you might imagine, your attendants feel honored to be a part of your wedding ceremony, but they're also keeping an eye on their own budgets.

If you want to have a destination wedding that will involve steep travel expenses, you should inform prospective attendants of the ceremony location before inviting them to be in the wedding party. That way your friends will know up front of potential costs before they get excited and agree, only to have to decline later when they realize they can't afford it.

Informing your attendants of the wedding date as far ahead as possible is vital so they can begin their own planning and budgeting. After close family members, they should be the first ones told of your wedding plans and the first to receive save-the-date cards.

You Can Control Some Expenses

One of the ways you can help your maid of honor and bridesmaids save is by choosing gowns that they can wear again. For a winter wedding, think about having beautiful cashmere twin sets and satin skirts. Spring? One spring wedding featured attendants dressed in white linen blouses tied at the waist and long floral skirts. For summer—spaghetti-strap dresses with pretty matching wraps.

 Essential

Try to find styles that don't require a lot of expensive alteration. One way to do this is to let each bridesmaid pick her own dress after you have selected a designer and a color. This way, each bridesmaid can choose the dress that fits her body and her style the best.

You can also help keep costs down by letting your attendants wear their own dress-appropriate shoes. Some brides want their attendants to wear dyed-to-match shoes, which can be expensive as well as not always a color they will wear again. How often will you wear a pair of peach-toned satin shoes or a pair of strappy silver sandals with three-inch heels if you're a casual kind of girl?

One bride wanted all of her attendants to join her at her favorite salon on her wedding day, and the price tag was stiff for most of them—particularly the mom of the flower girl, who never envisioned that she'd have to pay $30 to have her little girl's hair combed into a simple style with a bow.

 Alert

Think about treating your bridal attendants to a group session at the hairdresser's for a facial. It's great for relaxing and getting together with the girls before you become a married woman. Many salons offer a group rate—ask if yours does!

The groom can help his groomsmen save by not requiring that they rent their dress shoes from the tuxedo rental store, something the store personnel will try to emphasize they must do for a good look. The groomsmen will also appreciate wearing their own season-appropriate suits to a less formal wedding, saving on the cost of the tuxedo rental.

Inviting the wedding party to meals and special celebration dinners and making certain either that they do not pay or that the charges are very reasonable, will also be appreciated by the budget-conscious. Who wants to spend a lot on airfare and wedding attire, take time off from work, and then find that they must pull out their wallet for every meal—especially at expensive restaurants!

Timing It Right

The bride and groom can save their wedding party and guests a lot of money by setting the date early so that they can snatch the best airfare and hotel rates. If you have a lot of guests traveling from out of town, try to avoid peak travel times and all the expenses and hassles that go with them.

One bride was so caught up in planning for her wedding that she forgot all about the big balloon festival that took place in her town the week she planned to wed. When her mother, who lived out of town, ran into difficulty trying to book a room, she quickly alerted her daughter. The bride decided she didn't want to change the date, opting to let her guests know they could participate in the festival as a side activity to the wedding. She found a creative way to put up her guests, asking friends and family to help host visitors and to locate lesser-known hotels.

 Essential

Preparing welcome packets for out-of-town guests is a nice touch. You can ask the hotel or motel to hand them out to guests as they arrive. Include a list of local restaurants, movie theaters, attractions, and family activities, and throw in a few snack items and bottled water.

Check with your local chamber of commerce or visitor's bureau to learn whether there are any big events scheduled during the week of your wedding. This will ensure that your guests don't have a difficult time finding rooms or will have to end up paying dramatically marked-up rates. In addition, check with the hotel most guests will be staying at to make sure it can accommodate your guests. Hotels with conference centers often fill up with business clients, especially if there is a large corporate event scheduled.

Hotel and Travel Accommodations

It's almost certain that at least a few of your guests will be traveling to the wedding from out of town. Some couples pay for out-of-town guests' transportation and lodging, but this is entirely up to you. Travel expenses may include not only the airfare and hotel, but also the taxi, shuttle, or rental-car charges. It is a nice gesture and a good way to ensure your loved ones will be able to be there for your day, but it is expensive, especially for a couple on a strict budget. Fortunately, there are many ways for you to lessen the financial impact on your guests.

At the very least, provide your guests with the names and phone numbers of local hotels, motels, airlines, and transportation companies. This is a helpful money- and time-saving service that your guests will appreciate.

Hotel Rates

Whether you choose to pay for all of their expenses or not, you still need to provide your guests with information and options. You can arrange for special hotel rates for your wedding party, especially if you are using a particular hotel for your reception.

 Alert

Don't forget that an experienced travel agent can be a good resource for you and your guests. Be sure to inquire about hotel, airfare, or rental-car discounts if you have an auto club or other membership that offers discounts for travelers.

Select a place that is close to the ceremony and reception sites, and call to reserve a block of rooms at a reduced price. Ask whether the hotel will honor the discounted rate for guests who want to extend their visit a few days before or after the wedding. Make certain the wedding party and other guests know they must ask for the special rate by requesting the "Smith wedding party rate." Some hotels make it easy on you and your guests, creating a personalized Web site for you that your guests can visit to book hotel rooms directly.

Plan B

Be aware that while a hotel may be a wonderful location for your reception, its rooms might be pricey for some of your guests, especially if the week of your wedding is during peak season.

Have a few alternate choices you can offer those who need information on a place to stay. If you haven't visited these lodgings, ask friends or coworkers about them so you can save time checking them out personally. Some hotel reservation sites enable you to take a virtual tour of their rooms without leaving your home computer.

 Alert

American Airlines offers special discounts for wedding guests. If ten or more guests fly American Airlines to get to your wedding, they are eligible for a 5-percent savings on the lowest applicable airfare if you sign up for the discount.

Airfare Tips

Don't be in airfare denial—sometimes the longer you wait, the steeper the price. Airfares might zoom astronomically during certain times of the year—or seats might be totally unavailable. Remind guests to tie down their airline reservations. No one needs to pay extra because they waited to make reservations and your city hosted the NBA Finals the week of your wedding!

Rental Cars

Many of the large rental-car companies offer group discounts to wedding guests. Getting discounted rates for your guests might require a little effort on your end, but it's a welcome break to offer your guests. Go to the rental car Web site and submit a customer-service query or call the customer service number. You will receive a discount code to pass along to your guests. The discount varies depending on which size vehicle each guest reserves.

Gift Registries for All Budgets

We all know that you don't invite people to your wedding just to receive a present. Although your attendants and guests most likely would love to buy you a lavish wedding present, no doubt their budgets won't allow it. Luckily, you and your fiancé can help them choose presents that will satisfy everyone involved.

Register for Practical Gifts

First, consider what you really need. Do you and your fiancé have a lot of household items or are you just starting out? It's tempting to register for those fancier items you want so much, but if you have four rather threadbare towels between you, it's time to reconsider.

Here is a checklist of basic items you need if you're just starting a household:

- ❏ Cloth tablecloths and napkins
- ❏ Flatware
- ❏ Cookware
- ❏ Glassware
- ❏ Small kitchen appliances

Unless you have a practical everyday set of dishes or china, you'll want to put that down as an item in your registry with flatware that looks good with it. Make certain that you specify how many place settings—you probably won't need settings for a dozen, and your guests won't be happy if they hear you've returned the ones they bought.

Where to Register

If most of your guests live in the same city or town, it might be okay to register at one or two local stores. But if some of your guests live out of town, consider nationwide registries to help save them time and money.

Question?

What are the benefits to registering online?
It's hard to find any drawbacks to this, actually. You can browse a store Web site on your own before assembling a list. The list you come up with can be altered. Registering online enables you to access stores that aren't available in your area while offering a convenience to your guests.

Many large retailers—and even some local specialty stores—allow you to set up an online registry. You can register for gifts either online or by visiting the store in person, and your guests can view your registry and order gifts with a few mouse clicks. If guests are uncomfortable with ordering over the Internet, there are toll-free numbers listed for the customers' convenience. Amazon.com also features an online bridal registry, even though it doesn't have conventional stores. Wedding Web sites such as WeddingChannel.com and TheKnot.com allow guests to easily search the most common registries and find where you and your fiancé are registered.

Gift Alternatives

If you don't need or want anything for your nest, you can simply write "No gifts, please" on your invitation. If any guests still feel obliged to give you some kind of gift, offer them an alternative.

 Alert

It might be helpful to your guests to include gift-registry information on your wedding invitation, but wedding eti-quette experts advise couples not to do it. It's considered tacky and tactless.

Charitable Donations

You can let guests know you would prefer they donate to a charity in your name instead of giving you a gift. You can select your favorite charity or you can let guests choose a cause. The I Do Foundation (*www.idofound ation.com*) lets couples set up a charity registry online for selected charities. The organization also partners with numerous popular registry sites, including Cooking.com, JCPenny, REI, and Crate and Barrel, and up to 8 percent of each purchase goes to a charity of your choice.

Make It For Me?

If any of your guests are particularly skilled at making something you've always admired, don't be afraid to ask them for a handmade item you'd treasure much more than a store-bought gift. Perhaps you have a photographer in your family. While an entire wedding package might be a bit much to ask for, perhaps you could request an engagement portrait or something similar. Chances are, your photographer family member might be flattered enough to do your entire wedding and reception. It pays to ask.

If a family member or friend is a whiz at making fancy cakes, and you feel he'd do a good job for you (no amateurs on this important day!), tell him how much you would love for him to make your cake. Even though this requires a large time investment for the baker, the ingredients are not expensive. And this would be a huge savings for you.

 Essential

If your invitee is willing to make a wedding cake as a present to you, the job needn't be a daylong project. Your baker can make a simple layered, frosted cake to which you add fresh or silk flowers or a special cake topper.

Other possibilities for handmade gifts that can save your guests money—and show them how much you appreciate their handiwork—are fancy favors for the reception tables. With all the talk of wedding registries and store-bought gifts, perhaps your guests are too shy to think about offering something they've made. Tell them their handmade gift would be very special to you, worth so much more than any expensive gift they could buy!

Honeymoon Registry

Guests can contribute to a honeymoon registry in lieu of giving you a gift. You can book a honeymoon through a travel service or your destination itself and establish a registry. Generally, you pay for the essentials—airfare and lodging—when you book your honeymoon and register for extras for your guests to buy. Guests can donate a flat fee or purchase an experience, such as a snorkeling adventure, for you. Some sites also allow well-wishers to chip in for airfare or meals.

Personalized Wedding Web Sites

The personal Web sites couples create for their weddings even have a catchy name: "Wed sites."

What's in a Wed Site?

A Wed site contains a variety of information about an upcoming wedding, including a story of how the couple met, photos, directions to the wedding site, and links to area attractions and events. Such Web sites can be quite creative: Sometimes couples share funny stories about each other or visions of their future together. Some feature a time clock to show how many days, hours, minutes, and seconds are left until the "big event."

Visitors to a Wed site can R.S.V.P. online, let the bride and groom know what entrée they prefer at the reception meal, advise them of any special needs, find out at which hotel the wedding party has a group rate, and leave messages. Putting up a Wed site means you don't have to repeat the same information to all of your guests individually.

As a bonus, a wedding Web site enables you to save money on sending everyone pictures of the wedding and the honeymoon. You can upload digital pictures to your Web site immediately. You can even post a streaming video of your wedding for friends and family who missed it in person.

How Much Do You Spend to Save?

Prices for hosting your Web site will vary widely. Some are free, and others will run you more than a hundred dollars a month. Some sites require you to be a techie to set them up. Others are slick, easily assembled templates that require little from you beyond typing in some information and uploading pictures.

Before opting for a free or low-cost Web site, ask the owner these questions:

1. Will there be advertising on our site?

2. What kind of design options do we get?

3. When our site visitors R.S.V.P., will their e-mail addresses be harvested?

4. Can we set up links to other sites?

5. Are there interactive features such as maps? Message boards?

6. How much is this going to cost?

7. What kind of contract do we have to sign?

Here is a list of popular wedding Web site hosts:

- *www.myevent.com* charges a small monthly fee to host your wedding Web site. You supply them with information about your wedding, and they will create a Web site for you.
- *www.ourperfectday.com* provides all the services you need to create a wedding Web site for a small fee. You choose colors and fonts, supply information and photographs, and let someone else design and maintain your site.
- *www.theknot.com* is a free Web site service. You choose a design and add details about yourselves and your wedding day. Add-ons are available for purchase.
- *www.ewedding.com* is another free Web service that offers snappy, professional-grade designs and multiple options for sharing news about your special day with your friends and family.

Wedding Web sites are an inexpensive and convenient way to keep your guests in the loop as you prepare for your wedding day. They have a personal feel, and they are a fun forum to share ideas and get everyone pumped up. Some companies even offer interactive features like quizzes and polls.

Accommodations and Other Expenses Budget Worksheet

Use this handy worksheet to document potential expenses for your guests. Keeping track of everything your guests spend will give you an idea of how and where to save your guests money. You might want to make a copy of the worksheet and tuck it into your purse or daily calendar so you remember to make entries as soon as you make the purchases. You might need to customize this worksheet a bit, depending on your particular wedding plans.

Hotel accommodations for guests:	$_____
Meals:	$_____
Transportation:	$_____
Entertainment expenses:	$_____
Miscellaneous:	$_____
Total:	**$_____**

Chapter 14
Pre-Wedding Celebrations

The fun starts long before your wedding day. A wedding is too large an event to limit to one day. From engagement party and wedding shower to bachelor and bachelorette party and rehearsal dinner, you'll have plenty of opportunities to celebrate—which means plenty of expenses to budget.

The Engagement Party

It might seem counterintuitive, but holding an engagement party offers an opportunity to save money on your wedding. Wherever you decide to hold your wedding, there will likely be friends and family unable to travel there. If you are planning a small wedding, an engagement party affords a good way to include friends and associates you are not inviting to the wedding. An engagement party allows a wider circle of friends, associates, and extended family to share in your happiness.

 Alert

Be up-front about your wedding guest list. Tactfully make sure everyone at the engagement party knows that though you want to celebrate with them, you are having an intimate wedding ceremony. That way no feelings will be hurt when people don't receive a wedding invitation.

Another Party?

How can spending money on a party help you save money in the long run? Simple: Engagement parties don't require the expense of a wedding reception.

Engagement-party food can be simpler, the cake less elaborate (if you even want a cake), and you needn't worry about special flower arrangements or wedding favors. Better yet, you can hold the event in a private home so there's no need to pay to reserve a hall

When you combine an engagement party with a holiday celebration, the decorations can serve both occasions, and the holiday will put everyone in a celebratory mood. Many couples become engaged at Christmas or on Valentine's Day, festive occasions for an engagement party.

Making the Food Without Stressing Out

Save money by making as much of the food as you can, and save time and stress by keeping the menu simple and using shortcuts. Like barbecuing? Buy chicken when it's on sale at the grocery store, and stash it in the freezer. Brush on a homemade or bottled barbecue sauce and serve corn on the cob and pasta salad. Dessert? Serve apple pie or order a cake filled with ice cream and decorated with an icing picture of the happy couple.

 Fact

If you don't cook much or you're uncomfortable preparing food for a crowd, visit *www.allrecipes.com*. The Web site lists collections of recipes, enabling you to choose the type of food you want to serve.

Explore inexpensive catering options if you don't want the hassle of cooking for your guests. Many grocery stores and delis provide a catering service allowing you to reserve dishes ahead of time.

The Wedding Shower

Wedding showers mean additional expenses for the bride's close friends and family, many of whom will also be spending money to attend or participate in the wedding.

 Fact

People are getting married later in life, and many of them have already set up their own households; in fact, 59 percent of women now live alone and many own their own homes. They don't want or need presents—or, at least, the kind traditionally given at weddings.

Shower Etiquette

Showers are a snap for the bride. Your only responsibilities are providing the host with a guest list and showing up! Showers are usually held four to six weeks before the wedding itself. Only the bride's closest friends and family attend, and the guest list is typically around fifteen or twenty people.

If the shower is not a surprise, you can let your friends and relatives know that you want them to keep it simple for the sake of everyone's budget. Emphasize that the shower is an opportunity for making great memories and female bonding, which is far more important to you than expensive gifts or a fancy party.

Theme Showers

There are all sorts of clever bridal-shower ideas. One popular way to make showers more exciting is to introduce a theme. This way, it's not just another boring pre-wedding event.

Basket Shower

At a basket shower, each guest presents the bride with a themed basket. Most commonly, each basket holds items for a certain room in the house. For example, a kitchen basket can be lined with a pretty kitchen towel and filled with cooking utensils, pot holders, and recipe cards. Guests can be as inventive with the baskets as they want. A "first night at home" basket could include ready-made pasta, a jar of quality tomato sauce, a package of amaretto cookies, cappuccino mix, and a bottle of wine, all wrapped in a checked cloth.

 Question?

What about guests giving money?
Some guests do give a check or a gift certificate as a wedding shower gift, and that's certainly perfectly acceptable—sometimes even preferred. Never ask for money, but you can drop a subtle hint that you could use money to pay for wedding or honeymoon expenses.

Jack and Jill Shower

Invite the groom and his friends to a Jack and Jill shower. This joint affair lets the couple celebrate together. Customarily, the groom put in a cameo appearance at the shower to thank the guests, but it is becoming more common for grooms to attend the entire event. Inviting his friends and male family members makes it less awkward. Men are increasingly involved in their own showers, and a couples shower is a recognition of this fact.

Alert

Schedule these parties at least a few days before the wedding: You don't want the bride and groom to show up bleary-eyed at their own wedding!

Lingerie Shower

Perfect for the bride who already has all the bathroom towels she could ever ask for. Everyone can always use more lingerie! Make sure that everyone—especially the bride—is comfortable with this concept.

Bachelor and Bachelorette Parties

Bachelor and bachelorette parties are an opportunity to celebrate and mourn the betrothed's rapidly dwindling single days. Whether the party veers toward racy or tame, there are many ways to have a great celebration without spending a lot of money. Traditionally, the maid or matron of honor gives the bride her party, and the groom's best man gives his, but it's common for several people to take on the planning.

Couples parties are gaining in popularity. They are a memorable way to get both the groom's and bride's friends together, regardless of whether they know each other already.

Some Fun Ideas

A pajama party at someone's home is a budget-saving bachelorette party idea. Break out a bottle or two of champagne, rent some chick flicks, and pretend you're all at the spa with a basket of pampering goodies like facials and manicure items. Hire a belly dancer to teach all of you how to do the sensuous dance. You can find fun, inexpensive gifts for the bride—gag gifts are even better!

The groom will revel in a man's man bachelor party. Have a poker night complete with cigars and plenty of submarine sandwiches, potato chips, and beer. Give the groom the chance to participate with his friends in paintballing, camping, fishing, or a sport he enjoys.

For a couple's party, a wine-tasting event appeals to just about everyone. Check to see whether there is a winery near you or consider having the wine tasting at a restaurant. A wine tasting is surprisingly affordable since guests are only tasting various wines. This is a classy party theme that makes a festive couple send-off.

Have you and your fiancé ever been skydiving? If jumping out of a plane doesn't seem like a good idea just before the wedding, find a virtual skydiving facility near you. Everyone can experience the thrill of the jump with none of the worry.

Bachelor and bachelorette parties that take place on the town can be expensive. Partygoers tend to order alcoholic drinks on a tab without a thought to the one paying, making it easy for the budget to spiral out of control. Have your party at home, where you can be both comfortable and save money.

The Rehearsal Dinner

First of all, keep the rehearsal dinner in perspective: It's not a reception! Since you'll be spending a lot of time and money on the reception, you want that occasion to stand out among all the wedding festivities. It's best to pace yourself as far as the rehearsal dinner is concerned, since the main celebration is still to come.

Hosting Your Own Rehearsal Dinner

More couples are choosing to have their rehearsal dinners at the home of their parents or a close relative. It can be a challenge to get everyone together for the rehearsal, and you avoid feeling pressured to be on time for your restaurant reservation.

There's no rule that says the rehearsal dinner has to be at dinnertime. If you're having the rehearsal earlier in the day, make it a lunch or afternoon event. Sometimes, if the church or synagogue or other ceremony site isn't available earlier, the rehearsal will be done just before the wedding, so you could hold the rehearsal "dinner" whenever you choose, a day or two before. If you choose to hold the rehearsal dinner more than a day before the wedding, be aware that out-of-town guests may not be there in time.

 Question?

Who goes to a rehearsal dinner?
Everyone who is invited to the rehearsal, of course. That means those in the wedding party and their significant others, the parents of the bride and groom, the minister and spouse, and close friends and relatives, especially out-of-town ones.

The hosts will also be involved in the rehearsal, so you don't want them stressing over how they're going to get the food ready. They shouldn't be rushing off to put things on the table when they need to hear what to do on the wedding day—or worse yet, keeping everyone waiting when stomachs are rumbling!

DIY Dinner

Decide what type of mood you want to set. Your choice should be based on your tastes, budget, and the expected crowd. You can even host a gathering for dessert and coffee instead of a meal if you prefer.

Want something casual and inexpensive? Set out a buffet of sliced meats and cheeses from the deli with an assortment of breads and rolls, cold salads, lots of pickles and olives, and condiments. Add several types of fancy ice cream and sherbet for a refreshing finish to the meal.

Want a more elegant occasion? Whip up several fancy entrées or casserole dishes, such as a chicken-asparagus gratin or beef burgundy. Prepare and freeze these in advance, then thaw them in the refrigerator the day of the rehearsal. When you arrive home, serve your guests some simple appetizers or a tossed salad with several types of dressing while the casseroles heat. If there is a French or Italian bakery in your area, fancy bakery cookies make a tasty but budget-conscious dessert.

Alert

A buffet is easier on the hosts than a more formal sit-down dinner, but caterers and other food professionals will tell you that people will eat more food when they serve themselves from a buffet. Be sure to plan for this if you want to have a buffet!

Catering and Restaurant Options

Having the rehearsal meal at a restaurant or having it catered are two easy alternatives if your budget permits. It's best to work out a set menu if you're having a meal in a restaurant, because it'll save on the price and lessen aggravation. No one wants to get mad at Uncle Bert because he orders lobster when everyone else is being careful of your budget.

Ask the restaurant whether it has sample set menus that have worked for other events and discuss how you want alcohol offered. If you haven't eaten at the restaurant before, be sure to stop by and sample the food in advance of choosing the venue.

The caterer you hired for your wedding-reception meal may also provide you with your rehearsal meal. The advantages are obvious: You've already checked out this person or company and feel good about their service and food, and you may be able to work out a better price if they see they can get more business from you. Just make sure that the meal served for the rehearsal is sufficiently different from the reception meal.

Potluck

If you're part of a family that loves to cook, a potluck dinner can be a wonderful idea for your rehearsal dinner. Take this opportunity to connect with your culinary heritage.

In the weeks before the party, have one person keep a list of who's bringing what so you don't end up with too many desserts or entrées. Ask guests to write out the recipe for their dish and make enough photocopies for sharing. The happy couple can start their married life with a notebook of treasured family recipes, and other guests can have copies of recipes they admire.

Essential

One family found a free way to entertain guests at their rehearsal dinner. They set up equipment to play old home movies of the bride and groom as kids, and the two families bonded while watching their "babies" grow up.

Music Makes It Special

It's good to play appropriate music in the background of your pre-wedding parties, but there is no need to go to any extra expense. Ask friends and family to loan you CDs, and if there are any performers or "hams" in your group, let them entertain you.

Rehearsal Dinner Budget Worksheet

Use this handy worksheet to document expenses for your rehearsal dinner. Keeping track of everything you spend will ensure that you stay within your budget. You might want to make a copy of the worksheet and tuck it into your purse or daily calendar so you remember to make entries as soon as you make the purchases. You might need to customize this worksheet a bit, depending on your particular rehearsal plans.

Rental of party site:	$_____
Food:	$_____
Beverages:	$_____
Music:	$_____

Decorations:	$_____
Chair rental:	$_____
_____:	$_____
_____:	$_____
_____:	$_____
_____:	$_____

Total: $_____

Time Budget Worksheet

Keep track of what you have already done and what still needs to be completed for the rehearsal dinner with this worksheet.

To Do	Date Done	Deposit Made	Final Payment Made
Reserve rehearsal dinner site			
Put deposit down on catering			
Miscellaneous details			
Miscellaneous details			
Miscellaneous details			
Miscellaneous details			

Chapter 15
The Honeymoon of Your Dreams

Imagine—you and the love of your life on the vacation of your dreams, alone. It's your honeymoon, the relaxing interlude between hectic wedding planning and starting your life together in the real world. You've saved as much as you could and planned every aspect of your wedding and reception carefully, so now the two of you should have the honeymoon you've always wanted. Where you will go and what you will do is completely up to you—and your budget.

What Are You Dreaming Of?

The first step in planning a honeymoon is establishing your honeymoon style. This is especially important if you and your fiancé have never traveled together before. It helps to know at the planning stage that you are a beach bum while your fiancé is a museum-hopping globetrotter. Recognizing such differences ahead of time will help you plan a honeymoon that pleases both of you.

The Possibilities Are Endless

Sit down together one evening and do nothing but think about that honeymoon. If the two of you hold high-pressure jobs on top of the stress of planning your wedding and reception, you may want peace and relaxation. The image of the two of you sitting on a sunny beach, sipping margaritas, and thinking about absolutely nothing appeals to you. Maybe you can't pass up a chance to explore a new part of the world, or you want nothing more than to sightsee and shop in a big city. Regardless, make sure you and your fiancé agree on a honeymoon style; you may have to incorporate a bit of each person's dream vacation to come to a happy medium.

Instructional Honeymoons

Some couples seize the chance to learn new skills together on their honeymoon. Many ski lodges offer instruction if one or both of you has never skied. You can have active days zipping up and down the slopes and then spend those long winter nights in front of a blazing fire and cozying up in a big feather bed.

Cruises

A cruise is truly the getaway of getaways. You can relax on deck or take advantage of all the amenities of a luxury hotel complete with swimming pools, restaurants, lounges, planned activities you're free to enjoy or not, and shops. You can explore a new port of call every day or two and get off the ship for some sightseeing, snorkeling, or whatever you like.

The Caribbean remains a hot destination with honey-mooners. Jamaica, the Bahamas, Mexico, and St. Lucia are all favorite locales. Hawaii and Florida are popular tropical honeymoon locations in the United States. Las Vegas, New York, and San Francisco are prime sites for city-oriented honeymooners.

Some places are just naturally romantic and lend themselves to a honeymoon. But remember that it's the two of you who create the romance. The location and price have nothing to do with that!

What's Your Honeymoon Budget?

What kind of budget do you have for your honeymoon? Just as the wedding and reception budgets fall into modest, moderate, and luxurious categories, a honeymoon budget offers the same options.

A Modest Budget

If you are on a modest budget, try to compromise between what you want and what you can afford. For example, if you'd love to go to a tropical island but don't have the budget, think about visiting California, Florida, or Hilton Head in South Carolina and staying in one of the smaller beach towns.

 Alert

If time and money are short, consider a "minimoon." Take an abbreviated honeymoon at a nearby locale to get away. This will still give the two of you a chance to be alone and relax after the stress of planning a wedding.

Don't think of it as less than what you wanted. Think of the hassles you'll save yourself—passports aren't necessary! When you're sitting on a sandy beach, a mai tai in your hand, you may feel like you've found the island paradise for your budget.

Learn to Bargain

Most Americans aren't used to bargaining, except perhaps when they go car shopping. However, there is no reason for you not to seek a better deal on vacation accommodations. When Nick, our college graduate on a modest wedding budget, calculated what a bed-and-breakfast in a nearby state charged, he figured that he and Susan could afford to stay for five days. But they wanted to stay a week. So Nick called the bed-and-breakfast and explained his problem. And guess what? "They did it!" he enthused. "They never would have if I hadn't told them about the honeymoon and if I hadn't asked! It really helped us since we are students on a budget!"

 Essential

Play the honeymoon card. Many people are happy to help newlyweds celebrate. Ask your airline ticket agent for an upgrade to first class, and let the hotel check-in clerk know how much you'd appreciate a room upgrade. Even if officials can't accommodate your wishes, at least you will have tried.

A Moderate or Luxurious Budget

If you're like Kylie and Sean and your family is paying for much of your wedding, you may have a bit more to spend for your honeymoon. "We're going for one of those all-inclusive package deals in the Bahamas," said Kylie. "We found some great deals in the back of a bridal magazine, looked into it, and it's just what we wanted. It'll help stretch our budget for the honeymoon."

Essential

Check visitor's bureaus and tourist organizations for lists of hotels and motels. Compare the price of a rental condo with other types of accommodations. Some people prefer these because they can cook an occasional meal, or do a load of laundry.

Stretch your budget by not booking the best room in the best lodging in your location. After all, you're sure to be out and about so much, you won't care that you don't have the most deluxe accommodations. Reserve a portion of your budget for that unexpected special restaurant you spot or a gift you just can't resist in a little boutique you discover. Remember to set aside money for tips and unexpected expenses.

Timing Is Everything

Try to plan a vacation in the off-season. This strategy can save you money and aggravation. You'll also have more of the place to yourself to enjoy. One caveat: This doesn't work if you have your heart set on seasonal activities. If you want to go skiing, a June honeymoon in Aspen wouldn't make you happy.

Question?

How do I find out the peak season for a travel venue?
Just ask! Call the travel venue or visit its Web site. You can also contact a travel agent or check a travel guide.

Speaking of time, just how much time can you budget for a honeymoon? Often the answer depends on how much time you can take off from work. "Things are really busy around the time we're getting married, so we're taking just a week," said Lynn. "We've promised ourselves another week later this year."

Planning Ahead for Great Bargains

Planning a wedding six to twelve months ahead of the date gives you enough lead time to do some honeymoon pricing. The farther ahead you make those airline or train reservations and book that room, the more you'll save. With at least six months to plan ahead, you have plenty of time to research the Web for vacation ideas as well as bargain prices.

Be Aware

Does a particular travel deal sound too good to be true? Well, guess what—it probably is! There is perhaps no better time to remind you to put everything on a credit card and get everything in writing than when you make travel arrangements. No one needs to have a bad experience at such an important time as his or her honeymoon. It just sours everything to find that you've been gypped.

Be wary of any travel deal that is too aggressively marketed by a telemarketer or someone who represents himself as a travel professional. If he stresses urgency in booking, it's probably a scam. Take the time to check a company out with the Better Business Bureau or an accredited travel agent.

 Essential

Make sure your travel agent is a member of a recognized professional organization such as the American Society of Travel Agents (703-739-8739), the National Tour Association (606-226-4444), or the U.S. Tour Operators Association (212-599-6599).

Finally, check out what kind of weather is usual during the time period you'll be honeymooning. There's nothing worse than arriving in the Caribbean for two weeks of sun and sand only to have to turn around because a hurricane is bearing down on your island. Look into the weather and then make sure you have travel insurance.

Know the Add-Ons

A bargain room rate won't seem so great if you discover lots of little charges you hadn't expected. Advertised prices might refer only to the base rate; hotels can tack on tourist-trap surcharges and taxes that inflate the final price. Even if extra charges are legitimate, it's important to learn the total figure in advance to avoid price shock later.

Room service is a great perk—no need to go out when you don't want to, and it's understood that honeymooners usually don't want to the first day or two. But if you're watching your budget, you'll want to be very careful to use room service and the little minibar in the room judiciously.

Ten Ways to Save

Here are ten tips to keep in mind as you plan your honeymoon.

1. Time your honeymoon for a site's best rates. Call a hotel directly, because a hotel chain's toll-free operator might not know about special deals relevant to the hotel you're interested in. Also visit *www.hotelcoupons.com*, *www.hoteldiscounts.com*, or another Web site that offers similar services to get information about special deals.

2. Leave for the honeymoon during your air carrier's lowest rate period (usually midweek).

3. Don't eat all your meals in restaurants during your honeymoon. Cook some of them if you have a kitchenette, and make picnic breakfasts and lunches to take to the park or the beach.

4. The farther away the location, the more expensive. Staying within a few hundred miles of home will save you on airfare or gas.

5. Consider a package deal. Make sure the deal adds up to significant savings over purchasing all of the items à la carte.

6. Use one credit card to charge purchases for your wedding and accrue frequent-flier miles for your honeymoon airfare.

7. Check out bridal magazine honeymoon sections or visit *www.theknot.com* for information on honeymoon deals.

8. Two words: honeymoon registry. Guests can contribute to it instead of buying you a present for, say, the kitchen that you don't want or need.

9. Don't automatically choose the cheapest price on travel arrangements or you could make an expensive mistake. Examine the fine print on what the price includes very carefully.

10. There is such a thing as a "shoulder season." Booking your hotel during a time in between peak and nonpeak seasons will yield a price break. This period doesn't offer the savings of

nonpeak times, but it's still better than booking during peak times.

Fact

Disney World and Disneyland are popular sites with honeymooners because there are so many fun things to do and they offer so many different price categories.

When Things Go Wrong

So you've planned, researched, and picked your destination, bought the tickets, and made all the accommodations—and now you're committed. What happens if you are not happy with your vacation arrangements?

Remain Calm

You're on your honeymoon to relax and unwind, which can compound the frustration you feel when things don't go as planned. The first step in dealing with any negative situation is to stay calm. Find someone to talk to who can help you work out your issue. Explain what the problem is and mention you're on your honeymoon.

To minimize possible complications with reservations, always keep copies of your confirmation notices. If you are unsatisfied with the treatment you receive, get the names of the staff you dealt with and write a complaint to the parent company when you get home. It's possible to receive compensation even after your honeymoon is over. Always pay with a credit card so you can dispute the charges if you need to.

Hey, It Rained—Pay Up!

Travel insurance is crucial for making sure you are covered in case of problems. Your wedding insurance policy might cover your honeymoon, but it's a good idea to invest in travel insurance if you've opted not to purchase wedding insurance. As with all insurance policies, you have many options. Determine what you need. You should get a policy that at a minimum contains the following provisions:

- Honeymoon cancellation or interruption
- Lost or stolen baggage
- Travel delays
- Emergency assistance and evacuation
- Accident and illness coverage
- Bankruptcy of an airline or hotel

Ask your insurance carrier about policies or do some research on the Internet. Your travel agent is also a valuable source for finding reputable travel insurance. Even if you don't want to invest in a comprehensive travel insurance policy, look into individual insurance offered by the vendors you are contracting with, such as the cruise line, the car-rental agency, and the airline.

Focus on the Positive

Few occasions proceed flawlessly. When all is said and done, how you and your new spouse react to the ups and downs of your honeymoon is a life lesson. Try to take difficulties or unpleasantness in stride and not overreact. Your honeymoon might be the first trip you've taken together, but it won't be your last. Don't try to do everything, exhausting not only your budget but also your energies and good humor. If you love the setting of your honeymoon, promise each other that you'll return. The happiest married couples make time and save money for periodic special trips together, so as to renew their relationship on a regular basis.

Honeymoon Budget Worksheet

Honeymoon

Airfare:	$_____
Car rental:	$_____
Accommodations:	$_____
Food:	$_____
Entertainment:	$_____
Travel insurance:	$_____

Other

_____:	$_____
_____:	$_____
_____:	$_____
_____:	$_____

Total:	**$____**

Chapter 16
Creative Budget Ideas

There are so many great ideas to save money on your wedding that the first fifteen chapters couldn't contain them all. You can't close this book without these parting shots, these tips and treasures for saving you money on your way to the altar. So here it is, a compendium, a potpourri, a veritable goody basket of ideas to use!

The Thrill of the Hunt

"I think I had a real change of attitude about budgets and shopping for bargains after I went shopping with my favorite aunt the other day," a friend named Bridget said recently. "She has the money to buy what she wants, but I noticed that she went for the sale racks and bargain-shopped instead of paying full price. 'It's the thrill of the hunt,' she told me. 'If I find something I want at a bargain price, I've won, I've beaten the system.' I like that attitude. If I find ways to pay for something under my budgeted figure, I can then have that extra money for something really special that I want, or just bank the money and come out ahead for the honeymoon."

Become a Bargain Hunter

One woman who has some stunning art in her home shops at art festivals on Sunday afternoons, when the artists don't want to pack up their work and take it home. A flea-market bargain shopper using the same philosophy has bagged many items for less than their asking price.

How can this help you with wedding purchases? Since couples are encouraged to plan their weddings a year or more ahead, figure out what season will apply to your wedding purchases, then wait for the end-of-season sale. The big bridal stores run sales several times a year; check them out, but be sure it's a true sale and tags haven't been marked up in order to be marked down.

Fact

You can save hundreds and even thousands of dollars if you don't feel you must have the latest styles depicted in the fashion magazines. Besides, a good wedding-dress design should be timeless—rather than so trendy it will be out of fashion next year.

Look through racks of discontinued or last season's dresses. Remember that just because a manufacturer has decided to go in a different direction doesn't mean that last season's designs are now unfashionable. Years ago, after wedding dresses with huge, puffy sleeves were discontinued, there were plenty of brides delighted to look through the previous year's designs on the bargain rack.

The Fine Art of Negotiating

Negotiating is all about options: defining what you want, what you want to pay for what you want, and what you want to do if you don't get what you want.

It's very simple. Negotiating is about personal power, self-control, and sticking to your ultimate goal—saving on everything you can so you have the money for the special things you desire.

You Never Know Till You Ask

What many people don't realize is that shopkeepers and vendors are very often willing to negotiate on price.

Veteran shoppers of antique fairs, flea markets, and other places where bargains abound will tell you that vendors feel very vulnerable when the flow of customers slows and their merchandise isn't moving.

Part of the skill of negotiating lies in asking. You never know what you can get until you ask. Basically, there are two possible answers: yes and no. We've all dealt with rejection and lived through it, so know that if your offer is rejected you won't suffer a humiliating fate. Politely thank the vendor and move on.

The Negotiating Technique

Here is a simple way to negotiate. Approach the shopkeeper or vendor when she is not hassled by too many customers at once. If you notice she has just had an unpleasant conversation with a customer before you, use this to your advantage by smiling sympathetically and being extra courteous in your request.

Explain your situation—for example, that there is a stain on a dress you are interested in buying and you would like to get a discount on this damaged product. If it's an item that is dangerously out-of-season, like a swimsuit at the end of the summer or a summer wedding gown that is still on the rack long past the time a bride could wear it without shivering, then you should mention that fact. Have an idea in your head of how much you would like to see the item discounted. If the shopkeeper agrees, you've just saved yourself some money.

Alert

If you're not sure whether you can negotiate, practice with a friend until you feel more confident. It's a skill that will come in handy when you want a lower price from a caterer or a better deal on a honeymoon package.

If you receive a quote that isn't a bargain, express regret and name the amount you were hoping the price would be, adding that it will take X amount of time and money to make this item something you can use. If the item is expensive, be sure to mention that you are spending a lot of money. Also point out if you are a frequent customer.

If you don't get what you want a second time, ask very politely if there is anyone more senior who could authorize a price adjustment. If there is not an adjustment at this point, politely express regret, shake your head, and say that you're sorry, you just won't be able to take it. Turn and prepare to return the item to the rack or shelf. If you're with someone, say you guess you're just going to have to look elsewhere, so you'd both better be leaving now.

See what happens when you do this—you may well hear, "Wait, let me see what I can do," as you turn your back. Be gracious as they make another offer and see if you are happy with that. If not, decide whether you want the item or want to continue shopping.

Once you've tried this negotiating technique and had success, you'll never want to pay full price again.

Remember, the issue is not whether you're able to spend the money, it's that you don't want to. You'd rather spend the money you save on something else.

Bartering

If you have a skill or product that you can trade for something you want, take advantage of it. Bartering is, simply put, exchanging things rather than paying for them with money. I have something you want, and you have something I want, so we can exchange those things instead of paying each other. Why is this good? It's simple: Neither of us necessarily has money to pay for those things we want, but we have items we can trade for them.

A Lesson in Bartering

A neighbor approached an artist saying how much she liked a painting and wished she could afford to buy it. The artist appreciated the woman's enthusiasm for the painting and mentioned that he'd seen a coffee table she had made and thought she was a talented woodworker.

They looked at each other for a long moment, obviously thinking, until the artist offered to trade the woodworker the painting in return for the coffee table. Each walked away happy. That's an example of successful bartering.

Could you walk into a bridal store and barter with a saleswoman for a gown? Maybe not. But think about what goods and services you need and assess the possibility of bartering something that might benefit their owner, in turn saving both of you money.

How Can You Use Bartering?

The key to bartering is that the services or goods traded must be of equal value. You might be experienced with creating Web sites and can offer to create one in exchange for something a shopkeeper or vendor has to offer you. Perhaps the venue that will host your reception looks like it needs a service like painting or decorating, which you or your fiancé do. Not only might you save money on goods and services for your wedding, you might get some nice publicity or future business from the bartering opportunity.

Think about whether there is an opportunity and explore it mentally before you approach the other person so that you will be prepared to negotiate the barter. Use the same technique as for negotiating—except that instead of asking for a discount, you are offering to trade a service—or, if a complete swap of the item or service isn't possible, you can ask for a barter with some cash still exchanging hands. If you have a business card, you can always leave it with the shopkeeper or vendor so that they can think about your offer.

Bartering in Action

"I'm part-owner of a local print shop, and when I walked into the small hotel where we were thinking about having our wedding reception, I noticed that their menus and other printed materials looked dated and showed signs of age," a friend said. "I mentioned my work and asked if they'd consider reducing the price of our reception in exchange for some original, creative artwork and printing. They agreed, and we both walked away happy!"

Going Online for Services

The Internet is replete with money-saving resources for your wedding. The problem isn't finding a selection so much as finding the right ones. Make sure the deals you locate online are the best you can find and are from reliable sources.

 Fact

Thousands of vendors offering goods and services abound on the Internet. Being highly specific with your search is the best way to find what you want without spending hours at the computer.

Let Others Review for You

Use the experience of those in the wedding business or those who have arranged weddings to help you find what you need without spending a lot of time and money in your efforts. Look at online forums and heed the advice of wedding vendors and fellow brides and grooms who have preceded you. Take a look at wedding Web sites couples have posted and gather ideas for your own wedding plans. If you want to order invitations from a particular vendor, for instance, find an impartial, third-party Web site and read other couples' relevant ratings and advice.

Look Into It!

For information on everything you need to know about every aspect of planning a wedding, start with the wedding magazines and wedding vendors. Here's a list of some popular wedding Web sites:

- *www.theknot.com*
- *www.brides.com*
- *www.weddingchannel.com*
- *www.TodaysBride.com*
- *www.MarthaStewart.com/weddings*
- *www.wedfrugal.com*
- *www.blissweddings.com*

Essential

"The Dollar Stretcher" newsletter, available on *www .stretcher.com*, is a good source of money-saving ideas and suggestions from cost-conscious writers and contributors.

Get Specific

Looking for detailed ways to save for your wedding? There are many Web sites offering coupons and rebates on wedding items. Also consider saving on everyday items with the aim of putting aside those extra dollars for your wedding or honeymoon fund. One popular site is *www .coupon.com*.

Become an Educated Consumer

The better informed you are, the more money and time you'll save—not only on your wedding, but in every area of your life. Learning from the experiences of your friends and family as they navigated the wedding-planning highway can save you big bucks. Logging on to the Internet and scanning informational articles can be entertaining as well as informational. Comparison shopping and exploring other options can expand your understanding of what's available to you.

 Alert

To find a class near you, check out your local adult-education or community-education departments, community colleges and four-year universities, county extension departments, YMCAs and YWCAs, and so on.

Take a Course!

Have you explored the multitude of classes, workshops, and seminars available in your area? Even the smallest of towns usually has an educational institution available within a short driving distance. Some might even be free. Even if you've already taken required courses for a degree or for training at your workplace, it's an entirely different experience to learn without pressure, enjoyably.

Start with a course on better money management. There's no better time than when you're planning a wedding and preparing for married life. A class on learning how to budget pays off in increased money savings. You'll also develop an ability to set and achieve realistic goals, such as buying a home. Best of all, you'll encounter fewer disagreements over money with your fiancé.

Lessons for Wedding-Related Savings

Classes teach you new skills to apply to the do-it-yourself aspects of your wedding and are fun to take with your fiancé or a member of your wedding party. Taking a dance class with your fiancé is a fun way to spend time together and make sure you'll feel comfortable when all eyes are on you during your first dance. A flower arranging class could come in useful for making your bouquets and centerpieces. Other craft classes could teach you to make creative invitations or construct a wedding Web site. Fitness or self-defense courses will make you stronger and better able to handle stress at this hectic time in your life.

Fact

At *www.celebrityweddingsonline.com*, you can take a peek at the vows favorite celebrities used on their important day (actually, since most of them marry often, it should be days, right?). Choose the vows used by Kurt Cobain and Courtney Love, members of The Beatles, Julia Roberts, and more.

There are also classes that can bolster your relationship with your fiancé. A cooking class, whether it's to learn the basics, master new techniques, or gain an introduction to a new type of cuisine, can spice up the kitchen and create an area of mutual appreciation for the two of you. Classes on male/female relationships are fun to take together and will give you coping tools for your own relationship, too.

Free Prenuptial Advice

A prenuptial agreement is a practical arrangement that can save you money. After all, marriage is a business relationship as well as a romantic one. Neither of you wants to lose your belongings or good credit if you should ever decide to separate. Now, when you're in love and want the best for each other, is the right time for deciding how to handle a possible break one day, experts say. Celebrities and very wealthy people aren't the only ones who need prenuptial agreements.

Not talking about the need for a prenuptial agreement won't keep the reason you need one from happening, but avoiding it could cost you big later on. Don't be too scared to talk about this with your fiancé. Let's hope that once you draw up the agreement, you will never have to see it again!

The How Much Have You Saved? Worksheet

Now that you've budgeted for every item, use this worksheet to document what you've actually spent for your wedding. How much have you saved? You might need to customize this worksheet a bit, depending on your particular wedding plans.

EXPENSE	PLANNED	SPENT	SAVED
The essentials			
Wedding consultant:			
Ceremony site fee:			
Reception site food and beverages:			
Wedding cake:			
Cake knife, cake stand, and other utensils:			
Clothing for the bride			
Dress:			
Headpiece:			
Shoes:			

Undergarments and pantyhose:			
Hairdresser and makeup:			
Clothing for the groom			
Tux rental or purchase:			
Shoes:			
Underwear and socks:			
Stationery and postage			
Save-the-date cards:			
Invitations:			
Thank-you cards:			
Programs:			
Postage:			
Flowers			
Bridal bouquet:			
Attendants' bouquets:			
Corsages and boutonnieres:			
Ceremony site:			
Reception site:			
Miscellaneous:			
Music			
Ceremony site music:			
Reception site music:			
Other			
Transportation:			
Photography:			
Videography:			

Wedding favors and frills:			
Wedding party gifts:			
Tips:			
Fees			
Officiant:			
Marriage license:			
Blood tests:			
Miscellaneous			
Wedding insurance:			
Wedding party expenses:			
Wedding Web site:			
Entertainment expenses:			
Engagement dinner:			
Rehearsal dinner:			
Honeymoon			
Airfare:			
Car rental:			
Accommodations:			
Food:			
Entertainment:			
Travel insurance:			
Other			
Total			

Appendix A
Helpful Money-Saving Web Sites

There are many Web sites that help make budgeting easy and successful, whether you're budgeting for your wedding, your honeymoon, or your new married life.

Wedding Web sites:

Better Homes and Gardens Creative Collections magazine often features helpful tips for weddings at home and in the garden. Its Web site is *www.BHG.com*.

Brides.com is the Web site for *Brides*, *Modern Bride*, and *Elegant Bride* magazines. Save time and money finding local vendors and sharing money saving tips on the forum. Don't pay to have a wedding Web site set up; the site shows you how.

Martha Stewart's Web site, *www.marthastewart.com*, has hundreds of articles and photos to help you save time and money on your wedding and on making your first home together. Check out the budget tips.

Financial expert Suze Orman's Web site has eye-opening articles on the dynamics of money in a relationship. Read them at *www.suzeorman.com*.

The Knot (*www.theknot.com*) features an online budgeter to keep you on track and counts down the days to your wedding for you. Brides can personalize their budgets and find local resources.

Smart Couples Finish Rich author David Bach's Web site is *www.finishrich.com*. Bach has written bestselling books on financial success.

Index

Everything you need . . .

Trade Paperback, $9.95
ISBN 10: 1-58062-964-4
ISBN 13: 978-1-58062-964-5

Trade Paperback, $9.95
ISBN 10: 1-58062-982-2
ISBN 13: 978-1-58062-982-9

Trade Paperback, $9.95
ISBN 10: 1-59337-027-X
ISBN 13: 978-1-59337-027-5

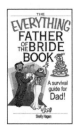

Trade Paperback, $9.95
ISBN 10: 1-59337-148-9
ISBN 13: 978-1-59337-148-7

Trade Paperback, $9.95
ISBN 10: 1-59337-057-1
ISBN 13: 978-1-59337-057-2

Trade Paperback, $9.95
ISBN 10: 1-59337-246-9
ISBN 13: 978-1-59337-246-0

Available wherever books are sold.